EMPOWER YOUR JOB SEARCH

KUNJAN VAISHNAV

A Book By:
FOREVER SHININGS
Instagram - @forevershinings.co
forevershinings1@gmail.com

Book Title: Empower Your Job Search

Book Author: Kunjan Vaishnav

Published By: FOREVER SHININGS

First Edition: 2025

ISBN: 978-93-7406-535-8

Disclaimer

The information presented in this book is intended for general guidance and informational purposes only. The job search strategies, techniques, and advice shared here are based on the author's personal experiences, research, and professional insights, but they may not apply universally to every individual or circumstance.

While every effort has been made to ensure accuracy, no guarantee is made regarding the success or results of any specific job search techniques outlined in this book, Job seekers should always consider their personal situation, industry- specific requirements, and consult professional experts when needed.

The author and publisher assume no responsibility for any loss or damage that may result from the use of this book's content. By following the recommendations in this book, you agree to take full responsibility for your actions and decisions during your job search process. Always approach your career goals with an open mind, flexibility, and a willingness to adapt to evolving opportunities.

ACKNOWLEDGEMENTS

This book is the result of the support, guidance, and encouragement of many remarkable people, and I am deeply grateful to each of you.

First and foremost, my heartfelt thanks to my wife, Shraddha, for your love, patience, and unwavering belief in me. Without your constant encouragement, this book would not have been possible.

To my mother, Jayshree Vaishnav, thank you for instilling in me the values of hard work, resilience, and kindness. Your wisdom continues to guide me every day.

To my parents-in-law, Vijay Adhia and Heena Adhia, thank you for your love and support, and for welcoming me into your family with open arms.

A special thanks to Mickey Mehra, my mentor, whose belief in me at the start of my career still resonates.

To Manjil Shilakar and Myriam Hasbi, your guidance has been invaluable, shaping me both professionally and personally.

To my dear friends, Abhijeet Singh Thakur and Swati Singh Thakur, for being my constant pillars of support—your belief in me has kept me going through the toughest moments.

And to the thousands of students, interns, and workshop participants I've had the privilege of working with—you inspire me every day. I hope this book serves as a guide on your journey, and I look forward to supporting more of you in future workshops and seminars.

To everyone who has been part of this journey, your influence and support have made this book possible. I am forever grateful.

INTRODUCTION

Searching for a job can feel like a daunting and endless task. With the right strategies, however, you can navigate the process with confidence, clarity, and a sense of purpose. This book is designed to empower you at every stage of your job search—whether you're building your personal brand, mastering interviews, or evaluating job offers.

Over the course of this book, you'll find practical steps, action plans, and insightful techniques for every part of the job search process. This isn't just about getting hired—it's about making choices that align with your long-term career goals and well-being.

I've distilled my experience working with job seekers into this comprehensive guide. By combining actionable advice with personal development principles, I've created a roadmap that will not only help you land a job but also develop the mindset needed for lasting career success.

About the Author

Kunjan Vaishnav is the founder and director of Aeron Skills Limited, a premier training organisation dedicated to empowering individuals and organisations to unlock their full potential. With years of experience in IT, self-development, and leadership training, Kunjan has made it his mission to help people overcome their limitations, build self-confidence, and navigate the complexities of personal and professional growth.

At Aeron Skills, Kunjan and his team offer result-oriented, practical training programs that cater to a wide range of needs—from job search strategies to enhancing leadership skills and personal development. Known for his dynamic approach, Kunjan speaks directly to people at their level, encouraging them to break through fears, gain clarity, and build momentum toward a successful future.

Kunjan's passion for learning and growth began at the age of 12, when he was recognised as the Youngest Trainer of India for delivering a lecture on the Bhagavad Geeta. Trained by internationally renowned mentors, he has since dedicated his life to helping others achieve holistic success through one-on-one coaching, seminars, workshops, and corporate events. Through Aeron Skills Limited, Kunjan continues to inspire thousands of individuals to not only succeed in their careers but to lead fulfilling lives, guided by purpose and confidence.

Kunjan is driven by a deep passion for learning and growth, and is committed to guiding individuals toward achieving holistic career success and personal fulfilment.

Index

Chapter 1: The Foundation of Your Job Search

Defining Your Career Goals

Defining your career goals is a fundamental step in the job search process. It requires introspection and a clear understanding of what you want to achieve in your professional life. Begin by identifying your values, passions, and strengths. This self-awareness will guide you in setting realistic and meaningful goals that resonate with your true self.

Once you have a grasp on your core values, consider where you envision your career heading in the next five to ten years. Envisioning your future helps you create a roadmap for your career journey. Break down your long-term vision into smaller, achievable milestones that can be tracked over time. This approach not only keeps you motivated but also allows you to celebrate small successes along the way.

It's crucial to remain flexible with your goals, as the job market and personal circumstances can change. Regularly reassess your goals and adjust them as necessary to align with your evolving aspirations. Engaging with a career coach, counsellor or even a recruitment agency can provide additional support and perspective, helping you to navigate these changes effectively while maintaining focus on your overall vision.

Networking plays a significant role in achieving your career goals. Connect with professionals in your desired field and seek mentorship opportunities.
These connections can provide insights and guidance that are invaluable in shaping your career path. Building a supportive network can also enhance your confidence and self-esteem as you pursue your objectives.

Finally, remember that defining your career goals is not just about achieving positions or salaries but about finding fulfilment and purpose in your work. Embrace the journey of self-discovery and professional growth. By aligning your career goals with your personal values and seeking continuous improvement, you empower yourself to create a fulfilling career that reflects who you are.

Understanding the Job Market

In today's dynamic and ever-changing job market, understanding its intricacies is vital for job seekers. The landscape has evolved significantly, influenced by technological advancements, economic shifts, and changing employer expectations. As a job seeker, recognising these trends can empower you to tailor your approach, enhancing your chances of success. This understanding goes beyond merely knowing what jobs are available; it encompasses the skills, behaviours, and strategies that are increasingly valued by employers across various industries.

Job seekers should first consider the importance of networking in this market. Building connections with professionals in your desired field can provide invaluable insights and opportunities. Engaging with like-minded people, being part of community groups, and recognised experts from industry can not only help you refine your job search strategies but also boost your confidence.

Networking can often lead to unadvertised job openings and allows you to gather information that may not be readily available through conventional job search methods.

Lending a helping hand by volunteering in the field of your expertise, guestspeaking engagements especially in schools and universities can open the doors to many opportunities.

Moreover, being adaptable and open to continuous learning is crucial in the current job environment. Employers are searching for candidates who demonstrate a growth mindset and the ability to learn new skills quickly. This is particularly relevant for those entering fields such as executive leadership or personal finance, where ongoing education and training can set you apart from other candidates. Emphasising your commitment to professional development can resonate well with potential employers, increasing your attractiveness as a candidate.

Understanding the emotional aspects of the job market is equally important. Job seeking can often be a stressful experience, and a positive mindset can significantly influence your success. Practicing mindfulness, relaxation, and stress management can provide techniques to maintain your composure and focus during this challenging time. Cultivating self-esteem and confidence will not only aid in interviews but also enhance your overall job search experience, making it more fulfilling and less daunting.

Finally, recognising the diverse roles within the job market can help you identify where your skills are best suited. Whether you are looking to become a leader, CEO, Managing Director, or a departmental head, understanding the specific demands of these roles is essential. Conducting thorough research and seeking guidance from those already established in these niches will allow you to align your career aspirations with market needs, ultimately leading to a more successful job search journey.

The Importance of a Positive Mindset

A positive mindset is a powerful tool for job seekers navigating the often challenging landscape of employment. When individuals approach their job search with optimism, they are more likely to stay motivated and resilient in the face of setbacks. This mental attitude helps to reduce stress and anxiety, allowing job seekers to focus on their strengths and capabilities rather than their fears and limitations. By cultivating a positive mindset, individuals can transform their job search experience into a more empowering journey.

Moreover, a positive mindset enhances overall well-being, which is crucial during the job-seeking process. Job seekers with a healthy outlook on life are better equipped to manage the emotional roller-coaster that comes with applying for jobs and attending interviews. They tend to practice self-care, which fosters both physical and mental health. This balance is essential not only for personal resilience but also for projecting confidence during interviews, making a positive impression on potential employers.

Developing a positive mindset also encourages proactive behaviour, which is vital in a competitive job market. When individuals believe in their ability to succeed, they are more likely to take initiative in their job searches.
This could mean networking more effectively, seeking out opportunities, or even acquiring new skills to enhance their employability. A proactive approach significantly increases the likelihood of finding the right job fit, reinforcing the belief that their efforts will yield positive results.

In addition, a positive mindset fosters better relationships, which can be instrumental in a job search. Job seekers who exude positivity are often more approachable and can naturally attract support from their networks, including friends, family, and professional contacts. These connections can lead to valuable opportunities and referrals. Furthermore, cultivating a positive attitude can improve interactions during interviews, helping candidates to build rapport with hiring managers and showcase their genuine interest in the role.

Finally, embracing the importance of a positive mindset can lead to long-term benefits beyond just landing a job. It instils a sense of purpose and direction that can guide individuals through their careers. As job seekers learn to maintain an optimistic outlook, they become more resilient in facing future challenges and uncertainties in their professional lives. This mindset not only aids in securing a job but also lays the groundwork for sustained success and fulfilment in their careers.

1. Defining Your Career Goals: Practical Steps

Step 1: Self-Assessment (Knowing Your Values, Passions, and Strengths)

Action: Reflect on these questions and write your answers down:

What values are most important to me in my career?
(e.g., creativity, flexibility, financial stability, helping others)

What tasks make me feel energized or fulfilled?
(e.g., solving problems, working in teams, leading projects)

What are my top skills and strengths?
(e.g., communication, analytical thinking, leadership}

Example: If you value work-life balance and creativity, then a role that allows flexible hours and innovative problem-solving (such as in a creative agency or startup} may align with your goals.

Tool: CliftonStrengths (formerly StrengthsFinder) is a great tool to identify your strengths, which can help guide your career direction.

Step 2: Long-Term Vision of your future and career

Action: Spend 30 minutes visualising your career 5-10 years from now. Ask yourself:

Where do I want to be in my career in 5 years?

What type of company or role excites me?

What lifestyle do I want my career to support? (e.g., remote work, travel, leadership roles)

Example: You might envision yourself as a senior project manager at a leading technological company, managing a global team, with the flexibility to work from anywhere and frequent travel opportunities.
Goal: Write a vision statement that reflects this. For example, "In 5 years, I will be leading a diverse team in a global company that values innovation and personal growth, while maintaining a healthy work-life balance:"

Step 3: Break Down Long-Term Goals into achievable milestones

Action: Once you've identified your vision, break it down into smaller, specific goals.

Year 1: Focus on building relevant skills. If you want to move into a managerial role, start by gaining leadership experience through volunteer roles or team projects.

Year 2: Expand your network. Attend at least one industry event per quarter, join Linked In groups, or take part in online forums.

Year 3: Take on leadership responsibilities at work or in your personal projects, and seek out a mentor.

Example: If your goal is to become a team leader, your milestones could look like:

Year 1: Complete a leadership training program.
Year 2: Lead a project or a small team.
Year 3: Apply for management roles.

Step 4: Seek Feedback (Mentorship & Guidance)

Action: Identify 2-3 mentors in your field and ask for feedback on your career path. Send a LinkedIn message or email asking for a quick call to discuss your goals. Sample messages:
"I admire your career path and would love to hear your insights on how you got to where you are today and any advice you might have for someone in my position."

"Hello [Name], I hope you're doing well. I've been following your work and really admire the progression of your career. As I'm currently navigating a similar path, I'd be grateful to hear how you managed to get to where you are today, and any advice you might have for someone starting out in this industry. Any insights would be greatly appreciated!"

"Kia ora [Name], I hope all is well with you! I have been following your work in [industry/field], and I am really inspired by the trajectory of your career. As I'm just starting out, I'd love to hear about the decisions or moments that shaped your career and any tips you might have for someone in my shoes. I'd really appreciate any insights!"

Example: A mentor in your field can provide guidance on what you should focus on next, whether it's gaining specific certifications, developing soft skills, or expanding your network.

2. Understanding the Job Market: Practical Steps

Step 1: Research Industry Trends

Action: Set aside 30 minutes per week to read industry news, trends, and reports. Use LinkedIn Insights to analyze which companies are hiring in your field and which skills are trending.
Set up Google Alerts for keywords like "emerging trends in [your industry]" or "growth in [your field]" to stay up to date on new developments.
Example: If you're in the technical or finance field, you might learn that artificial intelligence, machine learning and banking are rapidly growing sectors, and companies are actively seeking candidates with experience in these areas.

Step 2: Update Your Skillset

Action: Once you identify skills that are in high demand, take steps to improve them:

Skill Gap Example: If you want to move into digital marketing but lack experience with SEO, take a free course on Moz or Google Analytics to get up to speed.

Set a learning goal: Commit to finishing one course or certification every 3-4 months.

Tools: Some great resources for upskilling include:
LinkedIn Learning: Offers courses on a wide range of skills, from soft skills to technical skills.

Coursera: Partnered with universities for certifications in fields like business, sales, designing, programming, data science, management, etc.
edX: Another platform offering university-backed courses, especially in technology.

Step 3: Networking Strategy

Action: Dedicate 1hour per week to networking.Some ideas:
Linkedln: Personalize connection requests and aim to connect with at least 5 professionals in your field each week.
Industry Events: Attend at least one event (virtual or in-person) per month. This could be webinars, conferences, or networking meetups.

Informational Interviews: Schedule 1-2 per month with people in roles you're aiming for.

Example: If you're interested in a role in project management, reach out to professionals in similar positions and ask them how they got there. Try to engage in a conversation or organise a virtual coffee to have a casual chat to learn more about the industry and company. You can also lend a helping hand in their project work or offer to intern under their supervision.

Step 4: Stay Open to Opportunities

Action: Use job search engines to stay updated on new roles:
Set up Job Alerts on platforms like Indeed, Seek, TradeMe, Glassdoor, and Linkedln. Tailor these alerts based on location, job title, and skills.

Dedicate 1 hour each morning to reviewing new opportunities and applying to the ones that align with your career goals.

Example: If you're seeking a management role, look for positions that align with your leadership experience, even if they are slightly below your desired title. These roles may serve as stepping stones.

3. Cultivating a Positive Mindset: Practical Steps

Step 1: Daily Affirmations

Action: Start your morning with 5 affirmations to boost confidence and focus.
Write them out in a journal, say them out loud, or record yourself and listen to them during your commute.
Example Affirmation:

"I am confident in my skills and ready for the next step in my career:'
"Every challenge Iface brings me closer to my goals:'
"I attract opportunities that align with my values:'

Step 2: Practice Self-Care

Action: Incorporate self-care into your daily routine:
Exercise: Whether it's a walk, yoga, or gym session, aim for at least 30 minutes per day. This helps reduce stress and boosts your energy.
Mindfulness: Practice meditation or deep breathing exercises for 5-10 minutes daily. Apps like Headspace or Calm can guide you through quick sessions.

Example: Create a "self-care" calendar where you schedule personal time this could include anything from cooking a nice meal, taking a relaxing bath, or simply reading a book.

Step 3: Journal about your progress

Action: Create a habit of journaling at the end of each day to reflect on your journey.
Write about what went well today, what you learned, and how you felt.
Revisit your journal every week to track your progress and make adjustments to your goals as needed.
Example: "Today, I reached out to two new people in my network, and one of them responded positively about setting up a chat. I also applied for a job that I'm really excited about."

Step 4: Visualise Success

Action: Set aside 10 minutes once a week to do a visualisation exercise:
Close your eyes and imagine receiving a job offer. Picture the details: how you feel, what the company culture is like, who you're working with.
Picture yourself succeeding in this role and the positive impact it has on your career trajectory.

Example: Visualise your first day at the company, how you'll walk into the office with confidence and excitement, and the positive interactions you'll have with your new team.

Step 5: Celebrate Small Wins

Action: Recognize even the smallest achievements in your job search:

Did you have a great interview? Celebrate by treating yourself to a nice meal or taking time to relax.

Got a new connection? Celebrate by sharing it with a friend or posting about it on Linked In.

Example: After sending out 5 job applications in a week, reward yourself with a movie night or a fun activity you enjoy.

4. Putting It All Together: A 30-Day Job Search Plan

Week 1: Clarity and Self-Assessment

Complete your self-assessment.

Write your career vision statement.

Update your Linked In profile to reflect your career goals.

Week 2: Industry Research and Skill Development

Spend 30 minutes daily reading industry news.

Enroll in an online/physical course or workshop to develop a key skill.

Apply for at least 10 jobs.

Week 3: Networking and Mindset

Reach out to 5 professionals in your field for networking.

Start daily affirmations and journaling.

Apply for 5 more roles.

Week 4: Reflection and Adjustment

Reflect on your progress and adjust your strategy as needed.

Connect with mentors for feedback.

Continue networking and applying for jobs, maintaining a positive mindset

Chapter 1: The Foundation Of Your Job Search Journal

This section will guide you through practical exercises, reflections, and actionable steps to help define your career goals, understand the job market, and maintain a positive mindset during your job search. Use this journal to track your progress and make notes as you work through the various steps.

Section 1: Defining Your Career Goals

Step 1: Self-Assessment
Before you can set clear career goals, you need to understand yourself better. Reflect on your values, passions, and strengths.

What values are most important to you in your career?
(e.g., creativity, stability, helping others, independence)
Write your answer here:

What tasks or activities make you feel energized and fulfilled?
(e.g., problem-solving, teamwork, leading projects, hands-on work)
Write your answer here:

1. What are your top strengths or skills?
(e.g., communication, analytical thinking, leadership, technical expertise)
Write your answer here:

Step 2: Visualise Your Career in 5-10 Years

Take a moment to imagine where you want your career to be in the next 5-10 years. Think about the type of role, company, or lifestyle that would fulfills you.

Where do you want to be in 5 years?
Write your answer here:

2. What type of company or role excites you the most?
Write your answer here:

What kind of lifestyle do you want your career to support? (e.g., remote work, leadership roles, travel opportunities, work-life balance)
Write your answer here:

Vision Statement: Based on your answers, write a vision statement for your career in 5-10 years.
Example: "In 5 years, I will be a senior project manager at a leading tech company, working with a diverse team and having the flexibility to work remotely and travel."
Write your vision statement here:

Step 3: Break Down Your Long-Term Vision into Achievable Milestones

Once you have a long-term vision, break it down into smaller, actionable steps.

Year 1: What are your top priorities for building relevant skills?
Write your answer here:

Year 2: How will you expand your professional network?
Write your answer here:

Year 3: What leadership experiences or new responsibilities will you seek?
Write your answer here:

Step 4: Seek Feedback (Mentorship & Guidance)

Now that you've broken down your goals, it's time to seek feedback. Identify 2-3 mentors or people you admire in your field. Reach out to them for advice.

Who are 2-3 mentors or professionals you'd like to connect with?
Write their names and contact information here:

No.	Name of the mentor	Contact information	How this mentor can help?
1			
2			
3			
4			
5			

What specific advice or feedback do you want to ask them about your career?
Write your questions here:

Section 2: Understanding the Job Market

Step 1: Research Industry Trends

Stay informed about industry changes and trends to position yourself as a competitive candidate.

What industry trends are most relevant to your career path?

Write your answer here:

What new skills or knowledge are in high demand in your field?

Write your answer here:

Skills	Knowledge	How do I get these?	Time needed to acquire

Step 2: Update Your Skillset

Use the information you gathered in Step 1 to identify skill gaps and areas for improvement.

What skills do you need to develop to meet your career goals?

Write your answer here:

Skills	Knowledge	How do I get these?	Time needed to acquire

What online/offline courses/certifications, or internships will you pursue?

Write your answer here:

Course/Certification or Internship	What skills/knowledge would this provide?	How these meet prospect employer's need?	Time needed to complete

Step 3: Networking Strategy

Networking is crucial to gaining insights and opportunities.

Who can you reach out to for networking this week? Write names, job titles, or companies here:

How will you connect with these individuals?
Write your strategy here (e.g., LinkedIn, email, in-person events):

Step 4: Stay Open to Opportunities
Remain flexible and open to new opportunities that align with your career goals.

Where can you set up job alerts?
List platforms here (e.g., LinkedIn, Indeed, Glassdoor):

How often will you review and apply to new job opportunities?
Write your plan here (e.g., every morning for 1 hour):

Section 3: Cultivating a Positive Mindset

Step 1: Daily Affirmations

Start each day with a positive affirmation to set the tone for your job search.

Write your 5 daily affirmations below:

Example: "I am confident in my skills."

Affirmation 01	
Affirmation 02	
Affirmation 03	
Affirmation 04	
Affirmation 05	

Step 2: Practice Self-Care

Job searching can be stressful, so make sure you're taking care of your mind and body.

What self-care activities will you incorporate into your daily routine?

(e.g., exercise, meditation, healthy meals)

Write your answer here:

When will you dedicate time for self-care during the day?

Write your answer here:

Step 3: Journal about your progress
Tracking your thoughts, progress, and reflections is key to staying motivated.

What went well today in your job search?
Write your answer here:

What challenges did you face, and how can you overcome them?
Write your answer here:

What small win can you celebrate today?
Write your answer here:

Step 4: Visualise Success
Take time to visualise your future career success.

Imagine you've just received a job offer. How do you feel? What's the company like?
Write your answer here:

Visualise your first day at work. How will you walk into the office with confidence?
Write your answer here:

Step 5: Celebrate Small Wins
Acknowledge and reward yourself for any progress made, no matter how small.

What is your reward for a small achievement today?
Write your answer here:

Achievement	Reward for that achievement

At the end of this chapter, reflect on your journey so far. How do you feel about your progress? What did you learn about yourself and the job market? What steps will you continue to focus on as you move forward?

Use this journal as a tool to guide your career development, stay motivated, and keep track of your progress. By the end of this process, you'll have a clear path forward and a positive mindset to take on your next career challenge!

CHAPTER 2:
BUILDING SELF-CONFIDENCE

Identifying Your Strengths

Identifying your strengths is a crucial step in the job search process. It allows you to understand what you excel at and how these abilities can be leveraged to secure a position that aligns with your career aspirations. Self-awareness is the foundation of this journey, enabling you to articulate your unique value to potential employers. This process begins with introspection, where you reflect on your past experiences, achievements, and the skills you have developed over time.

One effective method of identifying strengths is to seek feedback from others. Engaging with friends, family, colleagues, or mentors can provide insights into your capabilities that you might not recognise yourself. They can highlight qualities you possess that make you a desirable candidate. Additionally, considering past successes in various roles can reveal patterns that point to your innate strengths, whether they be leadership, creativity, or problem-solving.

Furthermore, utilising assessments and tools designed for self-discovery can be highly beneficial. Personality tests, skills inventories, and strengths assessments offer structured ways to evaluate your competencies. By analysing the results, you can gain clarity on which areas to focus on during your job search. Remember, the goal is to align your strengths with the needs of the jobs you are interested in, increasing your chances of success.

It's also essential to consider how your strengths can contribute to the workplace culture of potential employers. As a job seeker, you should look for organisations that value the skills you bring to the table. For instance, if you excel in communication and interpersonal relationships, you might thrive in environments that emphasise teamwork and collaboration. Understanding this alignment not only helps in job applications but also in interviews, where you can confidently discuss how your strengths will benefit the organisation.

Ultimately, identifying your strengths empowers you to approach your job search with confidence. When you are clear about what you can offer, you can tailor your resume, cover letters, and interview responses to highlight these attributes effectively. This clarity not only enhances your self-esteem but also resonates with potential employers, making you a standout candidate. Embrace this journey of self-discovery as a vital part of your professional development, setting the stage for a fulfilling career ahead.

Overcoming Imposter Syndrome

Imposter syndrome is a common experience among job seekers, often leaving them feeling unworthy and doubting their abilities. This psychological pattern can hinder your job search and prevent you from showcasing your true potential. As you embark on the journey towards your next career opportunity, it is crucial to recognise these feelings and understand that they are not a reflection of your actual skills or experiences. Embracing your accomplishments, no matter how small, can help in combating these feelings of inadequacy.

One effective strategy for overcoming imposter syndrome is to reframe your thoughts. Instead of focusing on perceived failures or inadequacies, shift your perspective to acknowledge your strengths and successes. Keeping a journal of your achievements can serve as a tangible reminder of your capabilities. This practice not only boosts your self-esteem but also helps in establishing a positive mindset, which is essential during the often challenging job search process.

Another way to combat imposter syndrome is through seeking support from others. Engaging with an industry expert or a mentor can provide valuable insights and encouragement. Sharing your feelings with peers who may be experiencing similar challenges can foster a sense of community and alleviate feelings of isolation. Remember, you are not alone in this struggle; many successful individuals have faced similar doubts and have successfully navigated their careers by leaning on their support networks.

Mindfulness techniques can also play a significant role in overcoming imposter syndrome. Practicing mindfulness allows you to stay present and recognise negative thought patterns as they arise. Techniques such as meditation and deep breathing can help rewire your thoughts and reduce anxiety related to self-doubt. By incorporating these practices into your daily routine, you can create a more balanced mindset, making it easier to approach your job search with confidence.

Ultimately, overcoming imposter syndrome requires a combination of self reflection, support, and practical strategies. Acknowledge that feeling like an imposter is a common experience, but it does not define your worth or abilities. By actively working to challenge these thoughts and embracing your unique skills, you can empower yourself to pursue your job search with renewed confidence and enthusiasm. Remember, you have every right to succeed in your career journey, and believing in yourself is the first step towards achieving your goals.

Techniques for Boosting Self-Esteem

Boosting self-esteem is crucial for job seekers who wish to navigate the competitive landscape of employment with confidence. One effective technique is positive self-talk. By replacing negative thoughts with affirming statements, individuals can reshape their internal dialogue, which significantly influences their self-perception. Practising this daily can lead to a more optimistic outlook and enhance overall self-worth.

Another powerful method is visualisation. Job seekers can benefit from envisioning themselves succeeding in interviews or excelling in their roles. This mental rehearsal helps to establish a strong sense of capability and reduces anxiety about future challenges. By creating a vivid picture of success, individuals can reinforce their belief in their skills and potential.

Setting achievable goals is also vital for building self-esteem. Job seekers should break down their objectives into smaller, manageable tasks. Each completed task serves as a stepping stone, providing a sense of accomplishment and reinforcing a positive self-image. This iterative process allows individuals to experience success regularly, further boosting their confidence.

Seeking constructive feedback plays a significant role in self-esteem enhancement. By asking trusted friends or mentors for their perspectives, job seekers can gain insights into their strengths and areas for improvement. Embracing feedback as a tool for growth rather than criticism fosters resilience and encourages a more balanced self-view.

Lastly, mindfulness practices can help job seekers manage stress and improve their self-esteem. Techniques such as meditation and deep-breathing exercises promote self-awareness and acceptance. By staying present and focusing on the moment, individuals can reduce self-doubt and cultivate a healthier self-image, enabling them to approach their job search with renewed confidence and determination.

1. Building Confidence & Cultivating a Positive Mindset: Practical Steps

Step 1: Daily Affirmations

Action: Start each morning by speaking or writing down 3-5 affirmations that reinforce confidence and positivity. Examples:

"I am capable and prepared for opportunities that come my way:'
"I trust my skills and the value I bring:'
"I embrace challenges as chances to grow:'

Tool/Goal: Keep a small journal or use a notes app to write affirmations daily. Aim to build a routine where affirmations become as natural as brushing your teeth.

Step 2: Confidence Journal

Action: At the end of each day, write down 1-2 wins you achieved, no matter how small (e.g., sending an application, practicing interview answers, or even doing self-care).

Examples:

"Today I reached out to a former colleague for advice:'
"I completed a free online course module:'

Tool/Goal: Use a notebook or an app like Notion, OneNote, or Google Keep. Over time, this builds evidence of progress and reinforces self-belief.

Step 3: Visualisation Practice

Action: Spend 5-10 minutes once or twice a week visualising a successful job interview or first day at your new role. Imagine how you feel, act, and speak with confidence.

Example: Picture yourself walking into an interview, greeting the panel with a smile, and confidently sharing your achievements.

Tool/Goal: Guided visualisation apps (like Headspace, Calm, or YouTube meditations) can support this practice if you're new to it.

Step 4: Self-Care Routine

Action: Schedule at least 30 minutes daily for physical or mental self-care (exercise, reading, meditation, journaling, or creative activities).

Example:
A 20-minute morning walk
Yoga or stretching before bed.
Cooking a healthy meal as a form of mindfulness.

Tool/Goal: Use a calendar to block self-care time, treating it as a nonnegotiable appointment with yourself.

Step 5: Power Poses & Body Language

Action: Practice 2-3 minutes of power poses (e.g., standing tall with open posture) before important calls, interviews, or networking events.

Example: Standing with your feet firmly on the ground, hands on hips, and chest open helps project confidence.

Tool/Goal: Amy Cuddy's TED Talk "Your Body Language Shapes Who You Are" can be a helpful resource.

Step 6: Positive Input

Action: Surround yourself with confidence-boosting resources-read motivational books, listen to uplifting podcasts, or follow inspiring professionals online.

Example: Listen to a 15-minute motivational podcast during your commute or morning routine.

Tool/Goal: Curate a "confidence playlist" of your favorite podcasts, YouTube talks, or songs that make you feel empowered.

Step 7: Celebrate Small Wins

Action: Recognize achievements weekly, whether it's applying for jobs, making a new connection, or completing a learning module.

Example: Treat yourself to a coffee outing, share your progress with a friend, or take time for a hobby you enjoy.

Tool/Goal: Create a reward system to reinforce positive behaviour. This helps keep your motivation strong and your confidence growing.

2. Putting It All Together: A 30-Day Positivity Plan

Week 1: Laying the foundation (Daily Habits)

Day 1: Write 3 affirmations and recite them aloud.
Day 2: Start a confidence journal - write one recent win (big or small).
Day 3: Do a 10-minute visualisation of your future confident self.
Day 4: Take a 20-minute walk while focusing on positive thoughts.
Day 5: Work on body language and practice a power pose.
Day 6: Listen to a motivational podcast or audiobook or read a positive article.
Day 7: Reflect on your first week - journal what felt good and what you learned.

Week 2: Building Momentum (Inner + Outer Work)

Day 8: Write 5 affirmations that focus on your strengths.
Day 9: Journal 2 wins from the past week.
Day 10: Do a 10-minute visualisation of a successful job interview.

Day 11: Block 30 minutes for self-care (exercise, meditation, or creative activity).
Day 12: Practice power poses before a meeting or networking conversation.
Day 13: Read or listen to one chapter of a confidence-related book.
Day 14: Celebrate Week 2 progress - reward yourself for consistency.

Week 3: Expanding Confidence in Action

Day 15: Create a "confidence playlist" of uplifting songs/podcasts.
Day 16: Write affirmations around resilience (e.g., "I adapt and grow from challenges").
Day 17: Journal about a past success where you overcame fear.
Day 18: Do a visualisation of your first day in your dream role.
Day 19: Commit to a 20-minute exercise session.
Day 20: Use positive body language in a real-life interaction today.
Day 21: Reflect on how your mindset has shifted since Day 1.

Week 4: Strengthening & Maintaining Confidence

Day 22: Write 3 affirmations about your career future.
Day 23: Journal 3 wins from the past month.
Day 24: Do a visualisation of yourself presenting, leading, or mentoring.
Day 25: Schedule an hour for deep self-care (exercise, long walk, reading, etc.).
Day 26: Practice a power pose before a job application or interview prep.

Day 27: Share a motivational quote/post or reflection with a friend or on Linked In.
Day 28: Write a gratitude list of 5 things that build your confidence.
Day 29: Journal how your confidence has improved in 30 days.
Day 30: Celebrate your success! Treat yourself and set 3 confidence goals for the next month.

Chapter 2:
Overcoming Imposter Syndrome and Boosting Confidence Journal

Section 1: Understanding Imposter Syndrome

Step 1: Recognising Imposter Syndrome

Take a moment to identify the thoughts or situations where you feel like an imposter. Understanding when you experience imposter syndrome is the first step to overcoming it.

What situations make you feel like you're not good enough? (e.g., during job interviews, working on a team project, presenting your ideas)
Write your answer here:

How do these feelings of doubt or inadequacy hold you back in your career?
Write your answer here:

What are three recent accomplishments you've downplayed or failed to recognise) e.g., completing a project, receiving positive feedback from a colleague
Write your answer here:

Step 2: Reframing Negative Thoughts

Imposter syndrome feeds on negative self-talk. It's time to shift your mindset. Challenge those negative beliefs and replace them with empowering thoughts.

What negative belief do you have about yourself or your abilities right now?
(e.g., "I'm not qualified for this job," "I'm just lucky, not skilled")
Write your answer here:

How can you reframe this negative belief into a positive, empowering thought?
(e.g., "I've worked hard to develop my skills," "I earned this opportunity through my dedication.")
Write you answer here:

Write 3 positive, truthful statements about yourself that challenge your imposter thoughts:

1
2
3

Step 3: Celebrate Your Achievements

Celebrating small victories is crucial to boosting your confidence and counteracting imposter syndrome. Acknowledge your progress and successes—big or small.

What is one recent achievement, no matter how small, that you can celebrate today? (e.g., sending out job applications, learning a new skill, completing a task on time)
Write your answer here:

How will you celebrate this win? (e.g., take a break, treat yourself to something enjoyable, share the accomplishment with a friend)
Write your answer here:

Step 4: Seek Support from Others

Talking to others about your imposter syndrome can be incredibly reassuring. Seek feedback, advice, and support from people who inspire you.

Who are 2-3 people you can reach out to for support or mentorship?
Write their names and contact information here:

What specific advice or feedback will you ask them for regarding your career? (e.g., "How do you manage imposter syndrome?" "What can I do to become more confident in interviews?")
Write your questions here:

Section 2: Cultivating Confidence

Step 1: Daily Affirmations

Affirmations are powerful statements that can shift your mindset. Start each day with a positive affirmation to build confidence and eliminate self-doubt.

Write 5 affirmations that reflect your confidence and capabilities:

"I am capable of achieving my career goals."
"I trust in my skills and experience."
"I am worthy of success and recognition."
"I embrace challenges and grow from them."
"I am confident in my ability to learn and adapt."
Recite these affirmations aloud every morning. When will you dedicate time to do this?

(e.g., right after waking up, during breakfast, while commuting)
Write your plan here
:

Step 2: Visualisation Practice

Visualisation is a proven technique to increase confidence. By mentally rehearsing success, you train your brain to expect positive outcomes.

Take 5 minutes to visualise your success in a job interview or at work.

Imagine yourself speaking confidently, answering questions with ease, or leading a team.
Write down your visualisation:
What are you wearing? How do you feel in the moment? What's happening around you? (e.g., "I'm sitting confidently in the interview room, making eye contact, and answering questions clearly.")
Write your visualisation here:

Step 3: Building a Confidence Journal

Journaling is a simple but powerful tool to track your progress and remind yourself of your accomplishments.

What went well today in your job search or career growth? (e.g., you sent out applications, received a compliment from a colleague, learned something new) Write your answer here:

What challenges did you face, and how did you manage them? (e.g., feeling nervous about an interview, learning to adjust to new expectations)
Write your answer here:

What small win can you celebrate today? (e.g., completing a job application, following up with a recruiter)
Write your answer here:

Step 4: Mindfulness and Relaxation

Mindfulness helps you stay calm and focused during stressful moments. Incorporating these practices into your routine can help reduce anxiety and build confidence.

What mindfulness or relaxation practices will you incorporate into your job search? (e.g., deep breathing, meditation, yoga, nature walks)
Write your answer here:

When will you dedicate time for mindfulness or relaxation each day? (e.g., first thing in the morning, during lunch break, before bed)
Write your plan here:

Section 3: Building Resilience and Managing Setbacks

Step 1: Reframe Failures as Opportunities
Failures are an inevitable part of the journey. Instead of letting them discourage you, use them as learning experiences to build resilience.

Write down a recent setback or failure you've faced during your job search or career. (e.g., not getting a job offer, an interview that didn't go well)
Write your answer here:

What lesson did you learn from this experience?
Write your answer here:

What will you do differently next time to increase your chances of success?
Write your answer here:

Step 2: Cultivate Patience and Persistence

Job searching is often a marathon, not a sprint. Cultivating patience and persistence will help you avoid burnout and stay on track.

What are some ways you can practice patience in your job search? (e.g., setting realistic timelines, focusing on progress rather than results, celebrating small wins)
Write your answer here:

How will you maintain persistence despite setbacks or slow progress? (e.g., setting weekly goals, joining a support group, taking breaks when needed)
Write your answer here:

Step 3: Strengthen Emotional Resilience

Emotional resilience is essential to maintaining confidence through job search challenges. Strengthen this skill by engaging in activities that boost your emotional well-being.

What activities help you feel emotionally resilient and focused? (e.g., exercise, creative hobbies, socializing with friends)
Write your answer here:

How can you integrate these activities into your weekly routine?
Write your answer here:

Section 4: Putting It All Together - A 30-Day Confidence-Building Plan

Week 1: Recognising and Overcoming Imposter Syndrome

Identify moments of imposter syndrome and challenge your thoughts with affirmations.

Celebrate small wins and acknowledge your achievements.

Progress:
Imposter syndrome moments: ______________________
Celebrated wins: ________________________________

Week 2: Building Confidence and Shifting Mindset

Continue affirmations and visualisation daily.
Journal your progress and reflect on challenges overcome.

Progress:
Daily affirmations: ______________________________
Visualisation practice: ___________________________
Confidence journal: ______________________________

Week 3: Seeking Support and Cultivating Resilience

Reach out to a mentor or supportive person for advice.
Focus on reframing setbacks as learning experiences.

Progress:
Mentor outreach: ______________________________
Reframed setbacks: ____________________________

Week 4: Reflection and Adjustment

Reflect on your progress, celebrate achievements, and adjust your strategy.
Maintain persistence and patience through setbacks.

Progress:
Reflection: ___________________________________
Adjustments: __________________________________

Chapter 3: Crafting Your Personal Brand

Understanding Personal Branding

Personal branding is the art of defining and communicating your unique value to the world. For job seekers, especially those in training and coaching niches like life coaching, wellness, and executive leadership, establishing a strong personal brand is essential. It not only helps you stand out in a crowded job market but also reflects your professional identity and the expertise you offer. Understanding personal branding allows you to connect authentically with your audience, showcasing your skills and values effectively.

The first step in developing your personal brand is self-discovery. This involves recognising your strengths, values, and passions, which are crucial in shaping how you present yourself. Experts in various industries often convey their commitment to personal growth and resilience. You may come across such high profile individuals in networking events. By understanding what makes you unique, you can tailor your brand to resonate with potential clients and employers, highlighting your specialised skills in a meaningful way.

Next, it's important to create a consistent message across all platforms. Whether you are using social media, networking events, or your personal website, maintaining a unified brand image is key. For instance, a CEO or a Managing Director should ensure that their online presence reflects their expertise in their field, delivering results, improved revenue, fostering connections, and building trust. Consistency not only enhances recognition but also establishes credibility, making it easier for job seekers to be perceived as experts in their fields.

Creating an Impressive CV

Creating an impressive CV is crucial for job seekers, as it serves as the first impression to potential employers. A well-structured CV highlights your skills, experiences, and achievements, allowing you to stand out in a competitive job market. Start by tailoring your CV to the specific role you are applying for, ensuring that it aligns with the job description and showcases your relevant qualifications.

This targeted approach not only captures the attention of hiring managers but also demonstrates your genuine interest in the position. Remember, the role of the CV is not to give you the role but it's to open the door for an interview. Depending on the style of the CV and it's content, the decision would be made whether the candidate can be interviewed or not. The decision to give the job is yet to be made.

Networking plays a vital role in personal brandingparticularly for people in sales, finance, broking, coaching, etc. seeking to expand their reach. Engaging with others in your niche can open doors to opportunities and collaborations. Attending workshops, seminars, and online webinars allows you to build relationships with fellow industry experts and potential clients. Sharing insights and experiences can further enhance your brand, as it positions you as a thought leader and a go-to resource in your area of expertise.

Finally, personal branding is an ongoing process that requires reflection and adaptation. As trends in the industry evolve, so too should your brand. Regularly assessing your goals and the feedback you receive will help you stay relevant and aligned with your target audience. Embracing change and continuously developing your skills, such as in personal finance or productivity, learning new technical skills, will not only enhance your brand but also empower you in your job search, ultimately leading to greater success.

When crafting your CV, focus on clarity and conciseness. Use bullet points for easy readability and limit your CV to two pages. Begin with a strong personal statement that encapsulates your career goals and what you bring to the table. Follow this with sections detailing your work experience, education, and any additional skills or certifications. Remember, the aim is to provide a snapshot of your professional journey, so prioritise the most pertinent information.

In addition to job-specific details, also include soft skills such as communication, empathy, and problem-solving that are particularly valued in the roles like sales, technical support, medical representative, counsellor, scientist, etc. These attributes can distinguish you from other candidates and highlight your suitability for the vacant positions. Be sure to provide examples of how you have applied these skills in real-life situations, effectively illustrating your capabilities.

Visual presentation also plays a key role in creating an impressive CV. Use a clean and professional layout with consistent fonts and formatting. Avoid clutter and ensure that there is enough white space to make the document visually appealing. A well-organised CV not only makes it easier for employers to read but also reflects your attention to detail, a valuable trait in any professional.

Finally, don't underestimate the power of proofreading. Spelling and grammatical errors can undermine the professionalism of your CV. Consider asking a peer or a mentor to review your document, providing an objective perspective on its effectiveness. Remember, your CV is a marketing tool, and like any good advertisement, it should be polished and compelling to attract the right opportunities.

Optimising Your Online Presence

In today's digital age, optimising your online presence is crucial for job seekers, especially those in technical professions. A well-crafted online persona can distinguish you from other candidates and attract potential clients or employers. Start by ensuring your profiles on platforms like Linked In, Facebook, and Instagram reflect your professional ethos and the specific industry niche you operate within. This involves updating your bio, showcasing your qualifications, any certification, and sharing relevant content that highlights your expertise.

1. Crafting your personal brand: Practical Steps

Step 1: Self-Discovery for Personal Branding

Action: Spend time identifying your strengths, passions, and values to define your unique professional identity.

Example Questions to Reflect On:
What skills or qualities make me stand out in my field?
Which aspects of my work energise me the most?
What values are non-negotiable for me in my career?

Tool/Goal: Use personality or strengths assessments like CliftonStrengths or 16Personalities. Write a 1-2 sentence "personal brand statement" summarizing who you are and what you offer.

Step 2: Tailor Your CV to Reflect Your Brand

Action: Revise your CV to showcase your skills, experiences, and achievements that align with your career goals and personal brand.

Example: Highlight leadership experience, problem-solving, technical abilities and empathy for technical roles.

Include results-focused bullet points like: "Helped 10+ clients through digitalisation, achieving a 30% increase in productivity."

Tool/Goal: Limit your CV to 2 pages, use clear headings, bullet points, and a consistent professional layout. Have a mentor or peer review it for clarity and impact.

Step 3: Create a Strong Online Presence

Action: Update and optimise your profiles on Linked In and other professional networks to reflect your personal brand.

Example:
Linkedln headline:

Executive Engineer | Helping businesses complete projects in timely manner and transition from paper reporting to digital"

"Data Scientist" | Helping companies to transform raw data into actionable insights that drive better business decisions and improve efficiency.

Share insights, articles, or short posts relevant to your industry niche.

Tool/Goal: Ensure consistency across all platforms-use the same profile photo, bio, and messaging. Aim to post at least once a week to stay visible and active.

Step 4: Networking and Thought Leadership

Action: Connect with peers, mentors, and industry leaders to build relationships and credibility.

Example:
Attend webinars, workshops, or networking events.
Engage with others by commenting on posts, sharing insights, or offering help.
Tool/Goal: Set a target of reaching out to 3-5 new contacts per week or attending one industry event per month. Keep a simple tracker to monitor your networking efforts.

Step 5: Consistency across platforms

Action: Ensure your messaging, tone, and visual identity are consistent across all professional platforms and communications.

Example:
Use the same professional headshot across Linked In, website, and social media.
Maintain consistent language in your CV, Linkedln summary, and cover letters.

Tool/Goal: Create a mini "brand checklist" to review once a month, including profile pictures, bios, social media posts, and CV updates.

Step 6: Showcase Your Expertise

Action: Share insights, case studies, or tips related to your niche to establish authority and credibility.

Example:
Write a Linkedln article on management techniques pertaining to your niche.
Record a short-video demonstrating strategies or productivity hacks related to your niche.

Tool/Goal: Aim to share content at least 1-2 times per month to grow visibility and reinforce your personal brand.

Step 7: Reflect and Adapt

Action: Regularly evaluate your personal brand and adjust it as your skills, experience, or career goals evolve.

Example:
Ask mentors or colleagues for feedback on how your brand is perceived.
Update your CV and online profiles every 3-6 months to stay current.

Tool/Goal: Keep a personal branding journal to note insights, new achievements, and changes in your focus or niche.

2. Putting It All Together: A 30-Day Personal Brand Building plan

Week 1: Self-Discovery & Brand Foundation

Day 1: Write down your top 5 strengths and skills.
Day 2: List your core values and passions.
Day 3: Write a 1-2 sentence personal brand statement.
Day 4: Review past achievements and highlight 3 that showcase your unique value.
Day 5: Take a strengths/personality assessment (e.g, CliftonStrengths, 16Personalities).
Day 6: Journal how your strengths and values align with your career goals.
Day 7: Reflect on Week 1and refine your personal brand statement if needed.

Week 2: CV & Professional Profile Optimisation

Day 8: Update your CV headline and summary to reflect your personal brand.
Day 9: Tailor 3-5 bullet points in your work experience to highlight your key achievements.
Day 10: Add soft skills relevant to your niche (communication, empathy, leadership).
Day 11: Ensure your CV format is clean, professional, and consistent.
Day 12: Have a mentor or peer review your CV and provide feedback.
Day 13: Update your Linked In headline to match your personal brand.
Day 14: Refine your Linked In summary to include your brand statement and key achievements.

Week 3: Online Presence & Thought Leadership

Day 15: Upload a professional profile photo across Linkedln and other platforms.
Day 16: Write a short post on LinkedIn sharing an insight from your field.
Day 17: Share a relevant article or tip on social media to demonstrate expertise.
Day 18: Engage with 2-3 posts from peers or industry leaders, adding meaningful comments.
Day 19: Update your bio on all social platforms to reflect your niche and expertise.
Day 20: Join one relevant Linked In group or online community and introduce yourself.
Day 21: Reflect on Week 3 - note which content and engagement felt most authentic.

Week 4: Networking, Consistency & Growth

Day 22: Reach out to 2-3 professionals in your niche for advise or collaboration.
Day 23: Share a mini case study or success story from your work on LinkedIn.
Day 24: Review all online profiles for consistency in tone, messaging, and visuals.
Day 25: Ask a mentor or colleague for feedback on how your brand is perceived.
Day 26: Create a content calendar for the next month to maintain consistency.
Day 27: Post an original insight or tip in your field to reinforce thought leadership.
Day 28: Journal how your personal brand has evolved over the month.
Day 29: Identify 2-3 skills or areas to strengthen to make your brand more credible.

Day 30: Celebrate your progress! Refine your personal brand statement and set 3 goals for ongoing growth.

Chapter 3: Personal Branding Journal Personal Branding Journal: Building Your Unique Identity

Week 1: Self-Discovery & Brand Foundation

Day 1: Identifying Your Strengths and Skills

Action: Reflect on your top 5 strengths and skills that make you stand out in your field.
What are the top 5 strengths that set you apart in your profession?

Day 2: Defining Your Core Values and Passions

Action: List the core values and passions that drive you in your career.
What are the key values that guide your professional life?

What aspects of your work energise you the most?

Day 3: Crafting Your Personal Brand Statement

Action: Write a 1-2 sentence statement that sums up who you are, what you offer, and your unique value.
Personal Brand Statement:

Day 4: Reviewing Past Achievements

Action: Reflect on 5 major achievements in your career that showcase your unique value.

List 5 achievements that demonstrate your skills and value:

Day 5: Taking a Strengths/Personality Assessment

Action: Take an assessment like CliftonStrengths or 16Personalities to gain more clarity on your strengths and personality.

What insights did you gain from your assessment?

Day 6: Aligning Strengths & Values with Career Goals

Action: Journal how your strengths and values align with your career goals.

How do your strengths and values support your career direction?

Day 7: Refining Your Personal Brand Statement

Action: Review your brand statement from Day 3. Does it still feel aligned with your insights so far? Refine it if needed.

Updated Personal Brand Statement:

Week 2: CV & Professional Profile Optimisation

Day 8: Updating Your CV Headline and Summary

Action: Tailor your CV headline and summary to reflect your personal brand. Ensure they align with the value you offer.

What is your updated CV headline?
What does your CV summary now say about you?

Day 9: Tailoring Your Work Experience for Key Achievements

Action: Revise 3-5 bullet points in your work experience to highlight the most impactful achievements that support your personal brand.

Update your work experience with key accomplishments:

Day 10: Adding Soft Skills to Your CV

Action: Include soft skills like communication, empathy, and problem-solving that are relevant to your industry. Which soft skills will you emphasise on your CV?

Provide an example for each of these soft skills:

Example for communication:
Example for empathy:
Example for problem-solving:

Day 11: Finalising Your CV Layout

Action: Make sure your CV format is clean, professional, and consistent. Avoid clutter, and ensure there is enough white space.

Does your CV have a clean, professional design?
[ ] Yes
[ ] No
(If no, make adjustments here:)

Day 12: Peer/Mentor Review

Action: Ask a mentor or peer to review your CV and provide feedback.

What feedback did you receive on your CV?

Day 13: Updating Your LinkedIn Headline

Action: Update your LinkedIn headline to reflect your personal brand and career focus.
What is your new LinkedIn headline?

Day 14: Refining Your LinkedIn Summary

Action: Refine your LinkedIn summary to include your personal brand statement and key achievements.

What does your updated LinkedIn summary say?

Week 3: Online Presence & Thought Leadership

Day 15: Updating Your Profile Picture

Action: Upload a professional profile photo across LinkedIn and other platforms.

Do you have a professional, high-quality profile picture?
[ ] Yes
[ ] No
(If no, please get one)

Day 16: Writing Your First Insightful LinkedIn Post

Action: Write and post a short insight related to your field on LinkedIn to showcase your expertise.

What topic did you write about in your post?

Day 17: Sharing an Article or Tip

Action: Share a relevant article or tip on social media to demonstrate your expertise.

What did you share, and how did it reflect your personal brand?

Day 18: Engaging with Industry Content

Action: Engage with 2-3 posts from peers or industry leaders by adding meaningful comments.

Which posts did you engage with today?

What meaningful comment did you add?

Day 19: Updating Your Bio Across Social Platforms

Action: Ensure your bio on all social platforms reflects your niche and expertise.

What is your updated bio on each platform?

Platform	**Bio/headline**
LinkedIn	
Facebook	
X (Twitter)	
Instagram	

Day 20: Joining Relevant Groups or Communities

Action: Join one relevant LinkedIn group or online community related to your niche.

Which group/community did you join?

Day 21: Reflect on Week 3

Action: Reflect on the content you've shared and the engagement you've had. What felt authentic and aligned with your brand?

Which content and engagement felt the most aligned with your brand?

Week 4: Networking, Consistency & Growth

Day 22: Reaching Out to New Contacts

Action: Reach out to 2-3 professionals in your niche for advice or collaboration.

Who did you reach out to today, and what did you ask?

Day 23: Sharing a Success Story on LinkedIn

Action: Share a mini case study or success story from your work on LinkedIn.

What success story did you share?

Day 24: Reviewing Online Profile Consistency

Action: Review all your online profiles for consistency in tone, messaging, and visuals.

Is your messaging consistent across all platforms?
[ ] Yes
[ ] No
(If no, make adjustments here:)

Day 25: Seeking Feedback on Brand Perception

Action: Ask a mentor or colleague for feedback on how your personal brand is perceived.

What feedback did you receive on your personal brand?

Feedback 01:

Feedback 02:

Day 26: Creating a Content Calendar

Action: Create a content calendar for the next month to maintain consistency in posting and engagement.

What content will you share in the next month?

Day 27: Reinforcing Thought Leadership

Action: Post an original insight or tip that reinforces your expertise.

What original content did you share?

Day 28: Reflect on Your Progress

Action: Journal how your personal brand has evolved over the month.

How has your personal brand evolved over the past month?

Day 29: Identifying Areas for Improvement

Action: Identify 2-3 skills or areas you want to strengthen to make your brand even more credible.

What skills will you focus on next?

Day 30: Celebrate Your Progress

Action: Celebrate the progress you've made in building your personal brand and set 3 goals for ongoing growth.

What are your 3 goals for the next 3 months?

Sample Cover Letter & CV

Cover Letter & CV Journal for Job Applications

Section 1: Personal Branding Overview

Personal Brand Statement:

Write your 1-2 sentence personal brand statement that summarises your career focus, strengths, and value proposition.

Personal Brand Statement:

Section 2: CV Template

A. Personal Details

Full Name:
Email:
Phone Number:
LinkedIn Profile:
Website/Portfolio (if applicable):

B. Career Summary / Professional Profile

Action: Write a 2-3 sentence career summary that reflects your experience, skills, and what you aim to contribute to the company.

Career Summary:

C. Key Skills

Action: List your top 5-7 skills relevant to the position you're applying for. Focus on hard skills, soft skills, and industry-specific skills.

D. Professional Experience

Action: For each job experience, follow this format to highlight your achievements and impact in past roles. Tailor this section to match the requirements of the job you're applying for.

Job Title 1: [Scope of role]:

Company Name:
Employment Dates:
Location:
Responsibilities & Achievements:
Highlight any significant project contribution or a major outcome.

Job Title 2: [Scope of role]:

Company Name:
Company Name:
Employment Dates:
Location:
Responsibilities & Achievements:
Highlight any significant project contribution or a major outcome.

(Repeat for additional work experience)

E. Education & Certifications

Degree / Certification Name:
Institution Name:
Dates Attended:

Relevant Coursework or Projects:

F. Additional Skills & Interests

Action: List any additional relevant skills (technical tools, languages, certifications) and personal interests that can enhance your application.

Section 3: Cover Letter Template

A. Header (Company Name & Address)

Company Name:
Hiring Manager Name:
Company Address:
City, State, Zip Code:

B. Salutation

Dear [Hiring Manager's Name],
Respected [Hiring Manager's Name],
Honorable Sir/Madam, [In case of highly designated individual or a senior government officer]

C. Opening Paragraph: Why You're Writing

Action: State the position you're applying for and where you found the job listing. Include a sentence explaining why you're excited about the opportunity.

Opening Paragraph: I am writing to express my interest in the [Job Title] position at [Company Name], which I discovered through [Job Board/Company Website]. With my [X years of experience] in [Industry/Field], I am confident that my background in [Key Skill or Experience] makes me a strong candidate for this role.

D. Middle Paragraph(s): Why You're the Perfect Fit

Action: Explain why you are an ideal candidate for the job. Focus on your skills and accomplishments that match the job description.

Middle Paragraph:

In my previous role as [Job Title] at [Company Name], I [Achievement or Responsibility]. This experience allowed me to develop [Relevant Skill], which I believe aligns well with the responsibilities of the [Job Title] position at [Company Name]. Specifically, I [Example of how your experience matches the job requirements].

I can bring to the organisation my,
List of soft and hard skills
List core competencies required for the role you are applying for.

E. Closing Paragraph: Why You're Excited About the Role & Next Steps

Action: Reiterate your interest in the role and express your enthusiasm for the company. End with a call to action to schedule an interview.

Closing Paragraph:

I am excited about the opportunity to bring my skills in [Skill or Experience] to [Company Name]. I would welcome the chance to discuss how my background and expertise can contribute to the success of your team. Thank you for considering my application. I look forward to the possibility of meeting with you to further discuss how I can contribute to [Company Name].

F. Closing Signature

Yours Sincerely,
[Your Full Name]
[Phone Number]
[Email Address]

Section 4: Job Application Tracker

A. Position Details
Company Name:
Job Title:
Job Listing Source (e.g., LinkedIn, Company Website):
Application Deadline:

B. Submission Notes
Date of Application:
Status (e.g., Applied, Interview Scheduled, Follow-Up Sent):

Follow-Up Date:

C. Interview Prep

Company Research:

Common Interview Questions to Prepare For:

Question	Answer

Your Questions for the Interviewer:

Section 5: Review and Refinement Checklist

Before submitting your CV and cover letter, check off the following:

CV is tailored to the job description

Cover letter highlights key accomplishments relevant to the job

Proofread CV and cover letter for spelling/grammar errors

Ensure all contact details are correct and up to date

Verify LinkedIn profile matches CV

Have a friend or mentor review your application materials

If any specific certification, valid work visa, licenses or approvals are required for the position applying for, do attach those documents.

CHAPTER 4: NETWORKING FOR SUCCESS

The Power of Professional Relationships

In today's competitive job market, the power of professional relationships cannot be underestimated. Building a network of connections is not merely about exchanging business cards; it is about nurturing relationships that can lead to opportunities and support. For job seekers, these connections can be invaluable, providing insights into industry trends and potential job openings that may not be advertised. Cultivating a robust professional network can significantly enhance one's job search strategy, making it more effective and targeted.

Networking is not just about quantity; the quality of relationships matters tremendously. Engaging with professionals in your field fosters trust and mutual respect, which can open doors to mentorships and collaborations. Connecting with life coaches, wellness experts, industry specialists from your niche, or leadership mentors can provide guidance and enhance your employability. Each interaction can be an opportunity to learn and grow, not only in your job search but also in your personal and professional development.

Moreover, the importance of reciprocity in professional relationships cannot be overstated. When you offer support or share resources with others, it strengthens your connections and encourages them to assist you in return.

This mutual exchange is the foundation of a successful network. As a job seeker, being proactive in helping others can lead to unexpected opportunities, whether through referrals or recommendations that could propel your career forward.

Finally, leveraging technology can amplify the impact of your professional relationships. Social media platforms like Linked In enable job seekers to connect with industry leaders and like-minded professionals across the globe. Engaging with content relevant to your niche, sharing insights, and participating in discussions can elevate your visibility and establish you as a knowledgeable presence in your field. By maximising both traditional networking and modern technology, job seekers can harness the full power of professional relationships to achieve their career goals.

Emotional intelligence plays a crucial role in forging these connections. Understanding the needs and motivations of others allows you to engage meaningfully and identify ways to contribute positively to their professional lives. Skills developed in finance, technology, sales, marketing, management, etc. can enhance your interactions, making you a more empathetic and effective networker. This not only helps in building lasting relationships but also increases your confidence in navigating social situations.

Effective Networking Strategies

Effective networking strategies are crucial for job seekers who are aiming to enhance their career prospects. Building a strong professional network can provide valuable insights, opportunities, and support during a job search.

One of the foundational strategies is to identify and engage with industry-specific groups, whether they are online forums, local meet-ups, or professional associations. This targeted approach ensures that job seekers connect with individuals who can offer relevant advice and potential job leads.

Another key strategy involves leveraging social media platforms such as LinkedIn. Job seekers should optimise their profiles to reflect their skills, experiences, and aspirations. Engaging with content related to their field, sharing insights, and connecting with industry leaders can significantly increase visibility and credibility. Moreover, initiating conversations with connections can lead to unexpected opportunities and collaborations.

Attending networking events and workshops is also an effective way to meet new contacts. These events provide an environment where job seekers can practice their interpersonal skills and gain confidence in their networking abilities.

Preparing a personal elevator pitch can help articulate one's professional story succinctly, making it easier to make lasting impressions on potential e
mployers or mentors.

Following up with new contacts after initial meetings is essential for maintaining relationships. Sending a personalised thank-you message or sharing an article relevant to the conversation can keep the connection alive. This practice not only demonstrates professionalism but also shows genuine interest in the relationship, paving the way for future interactions and support.

Lastly, job seekers should be open to giving back to their network. Offering assistance, whether through sharing resources or providing insights, helps to create a reciprocal relationship. By actively contributing to their network, job seekers can foster a sense of community and trust, making it more likely that others will reciprocate when they are in need of support or job referrals.

Leveraging Social Media for Connections

In today's digital age, social media has become an essential tool for job seekers to connect with potential employers, industry leaders, and like-minded professionals. Platforms such as LinkedIn, Twitter, and Facebook provide unique opportunities to showcase your skills and experiences while expanding your network. By strategically utilising these platforms, you can enhance your visibility and significantly improve your chances of landing your dream job. It's important to approach social media not just as a way to seek employment, but as a powerful networking tool that can lead to meaningful connections.

To leverage social media effectively, begin by optimising your profiles. Ensure that your Linked In profile is complete with a professional photo, a compelling headline, and a detailed summary highlighting your accomplishments and skills. Use keywords relevant to your industry to make it easier for recruiters to find you.

Additionally, showcase your expertise by sharing articles, insights, and engaging with others in your field. This not only establishes you as a knowledgeable professional but also invites others to connect with you, creating a robust professional network.

Engagement is key in building connections on social media. Participate in discussions, comment on posts, and share content that resonates with your professional goals. This active participation demonstrates your interest and enthusiasm, making it more likely for others to reciprocate. Joining industry specific groups on platforms like Facebook or Linked In can also provide you with valuable networking opportunities, allowing you to engage with peers and industry leaders directly.

Moreover, consider reaching out to individuals directly with personalised messages. Whether it's a former colleague, a mentor, or someone you admire in your field, don't hesitate to initiate conversations. A thoughtful message expressing your interest in their work can lead to valuable connections and insights. Remember, building relationships takes time; be patient and consistent in your efforts to engage and connect with others.

Lastly, maintain a professional image across all your social media platforms. Potential employers often review candidates' online presence, so ensure that your profiles reflect your professional brand. Avoid sharing content that could be deemed inappropriate or unprofessional. By presenting yourself positively and authentically, you will attract the right connections and opportunities that align with your career aspirations.

1. Networking for Success: Practical Steps

Step 1: Map your Network

Action: Identify people you already know who could support your career - mentors, colleagues, former classmates, or industry peers.

Example: Make a list of 20 contacts, noting how they are connected to your field and what kind of support they could offer.

Tool/Goal: Use a simple spreadsheet or notebook to track names, contact info, and potential ways to engage with them.

Step 2: Craft Your Elevator Pitch

Action: Prepare a concise 30-60 second introduction that highlights who you are, what you do, and your goals.

Example: "Hi, I'm [Name], specialising in [my professional niche]. I help clients [challenges for your niche] with practical strategies. I'm currently expanding my network in this field and would love to connect with others interested in professional growth:'

Tool/Goal: Practice your pitch aloud until it feels natural and confident. Record yourself to refine delivery.

Step 3: Engage in Networking Events

Action: Attend in-person or virtual events related to your industry.

Example: Webinars, conferences, workshops, or meet-ups relevant to your professional coaching, niche, technical subject, leadership, or personal development.

Tool/Goal: Aim to attend at least one event per week or four per month. Take notes on key contacts and insights.

Step 4: Leverage Social Media Strategically

Action: Optimise your Linkedln (or other relevant platforms) and actively engage with content in your niche.

Example: Update your profile headline and summary to reflect your expertise. Share insights, comment thoughtfully on posts, or join relevant groups.

Tool/Goal: Post or engage with content at least 2-3 times per week to stay visible and build credibility.

Step 5: Initiate Connections

Action: Reach out to new or existing contacts with personalised messages.

Example Messages:
"Hi [Name], I enjoyed your recent article on stress management. I'd love to connect and learn more about your approach:'
"Hello [Name], I'm expanding my network in [your industry] and would value your advice on career growth in this field:'

Tool/Goal: Target 2-3 new connection requests per week. Keep a record of who you contacted and any follow-up notes.

Step 6: Follow Up & Maintain Relationships

Action: Send personalised follow-up messages after meetings, events, or introductions.

Example:
"Thank you for your time today, [Name]. I appreciated your insights and look forward to staying in touch!"
Share relevant articles or resources with contacts you've recently met.

Tool/Goal: Set reminders to follow up within 48 hours after a meeting or networking event.

Step 7: Offer Value & Reciprocity

Action: Help others in your network by sharing resources, introducing contacts, or offering support.

Example:
Connect two contacts who could benefit from each other.
Share a free resource or article relevant to their interests.

Tool/Goal: Aim to contribute value to at least one person per week. Reciprocity strengthens relationships and builds trust.

Step 8: Reflect and Refine

Action: Review your networking efforts weekly and adjust your strategy.

Example:
Which events or connections were most valuable?
How can you improve your engagement or follow-up practices?

Tool/Goal: Maintain a networking journal to track contacts, interactions, and lessons learned. Use this to plan next week's outreach.

2. Putting It All Together: A 30-Day Networking building plan

Week 1: Mapping & Preparing

Day 1: Make a list of 20 existing contacts (mentors, colleagues, peers).
Day 2: Identify 5 new professionals you want to connect with.
Day 3: Draft your personal elevator pitch.
Day 4: Practice your pitch aloud or record yourself.
Day 5: Review your Linkedln profile and ensure your headline reflects your expertise.
Day 6: Optimise your Linked In summary and key skills to match your career goals.
Day 7: Reflect on Week 1and refine your pitch and Linked In profile as needed.

Week 2: Reaching Out & Engaging

Day 8: Send 2-3 personalised connection requests on Linked In.
Day 9: Comment thoughtfully on 2-3 posts in your industry.
Day 10: Share one article or insight on Linked In relevant to your niche.
Day 11: Send a personalised message to a mentor or peer for advice.
Day 12: Research one upcoming networking event (virtual or in-person).
Day 13: Prepare 2-3 questions to ask during networking conversations.
Day 14: Reflect on Week 2-note which connections were most engaging.

Week 3: Attending & Following Up

Day 15: Attend a networking event, webinar, or online workshop.
Day 16: Send follow-up messages to people you met at events or online.
Day 17: Reach out to one new professional in your field with a personalised message.
Day 18: Share a helpful resource, article, or tip with a contact in your network.
Day 19: Comment on at least 3 posts by industry leaders.
Day 20: Practice your elevator pitch in a real conversation (online or offline).
Day 21: Reflect on Week 3-journal which strategies built the strongest connections.

Week 4: Strengthening Relationships & Offering Value
Day 22: Offer to introduce two contacts who could help each other.
Day 23: Share a success story or tip in your niche on Linked In.
Day 24: Schedule a 15-minute informational call with a professional in your field.
Day 25: Send a thank-you note to someone who recently helped or advised you.
Day 26: Engage in a discussion in an industry group or forum.
Day 27: Identify one skill you can offer to help someone in your network.
Day 28: Review all your new connections and organise them in a contact tracker.
Day 29: Journal the progress you've made in building your network.
Day 30: Celebrate your achievements! Set 3 networking goals for the next mont

Chapter 4: Networking for Success: Journal for Building Professional Relationships

Networking is a powerful tool that can enhance your career prospects by opening doors to new opportunities, knowledge, and connections. In this chapter, you will create a personalised plan to build and nurture meaningful professional relationships. Whether you're starting from scratch or looking to improve your existing network, this journal will guide you through actionable steps to maximise your networking potential.

Section 1: Mapping Your Network

Step 1: Identify Your Existing Contacts

Action: Start by listing 20 people you already know who can support your career. These could be mentors, colleagues, former classmates, or industry peers.

Name:

Relationship/Connection to You:
How They Can Support You:

Example Contacts to Consider:

Mentor from past job:
Industry colleague you met at a conference:
Former manager who knows your work ethic:
University professor or advisor:
Industry association leader:
Former co-worker who's now in a senior position:

Reflection:

Do you have a diverse range of contacts from different areas of your career?

Is there someone in your network who could connect you to opportunities you haven't yet considered?

Step 2: Craft Your Elevator Pitch

Action: Write a concise 30-60 second elevator pitch. This should highlight who you are, what you do, and your career goals.

Elevator Pitch:

Practice:

Recite your pitch aloud until it feels natural.
Record yourself and assess your delivery.
Fine-tune it based on feedback or how you feel about it.

Reflection:

Does your pitch sound authentic and confident?
Is it aligned with your professional goals?
How can you improve your delivery or wording?

Section 2: Engaging in Networking Activities

Step 3: Attend Networking Events & Workshops

Action: Identify at least one networking event (virtual or in-person) to attend this week.

Event Name:
Date and Time:
Key Takeaways / People Met:

Reflection:

Did you feel comfortable engaging with others at the event?
What insights did you gain?
Who did you meet that could become a valuable contact?

Step 4: Leverage Social Media Strategically

Action: Update and optimise your LinkedIn profile. Ensure it reflects your professional experience, goals, and expertise.

Profile Headline:

Profile Summary:

Engagement Goal:

Post/share relevant content at least 2-3 times per week.
Comment thoughtfully on posts from industry leaders or peers.

Reflection:

Is your LinkedIn profile optimised for the roles you're targeting?
Have you shared anything that showcases your expertise in your field recently?

Section 3: Initiating & Strengthening Connections

Step 5: Reach Out to New Contacts

Action: This week, initiate 2-3 new connections with personalised messages. Think about people you admire in your field or colleagues who can offer new perspectives.

Example Message 1:
"Hi [Name], I recently came across your article on [topic]. I loved your insights and would love to connect with you to exchange ideas on [related subject]."

Example Message 2:
"Hello [Name], I'm expanding my network in [your industry], and your experience with [specific role/skill] really resonates with my current career goals. I'd love to connect and learn more from your journey."

Person/Contact:
Message Sent Date:
Follow-Up Notes:

Person/Contact/Designation/Current organisation:
Message Sent:
Date when message sent:
Response Received:
Follow up Notes:

Reflection:

Did you tailor your message to the person's work/interests?
How did you feel about initiating these new connections?

Step 6: Follow Up & Maintain Relationships

Action: After your initial outreach or meeting, send a follow-up message to keep the relationship active.

Follow-Up Message Example:
"Hi [Name], it was great connecting with you at [event/meeting]. I enjoyed our conversation about [topic]. I look forward to staying in touch and sharing resources that might interest you!"

Person Contacted:
Follow-Up Message Sent Date:

Reflection:

Did the follow-up strengthen the relationship?

How did the recipient respond?

Were there any action steps or further opportunities discussed?

Section 4: Offering Value & Reciprocity

Step 7: Contribute Value to Your Network

Action: Offer support or share valuable resources with your network. Aim to help at least one person this week by providing an article, making an introduction, or sharing a piece of advice.

Person Helped:

Action Taken (e.g., shared resource, made introduction):

Reflection:

How did you feel about helping others in your network?
Did this strengthen the connection?
Are there opportunities where you can continue offering value?

Section 5: Reflecting & Refining Your Strategy

Step 8: Weekly Reflection & Refinement

Action: Take a moment each week to reflect on your networking efforts. What worked well? What areas can you improve on?

Reflection Prompts:

Which connections were most valuable?

What strategies helped you feel more confident and effective in your networking?

What are your next steps in reaching out or building stronger relationships?

Reflection Notes:

Section 6: 30-Day Networking Plan

Week 1: Mapping & Preparing

Day 1: Make a list of 20 existing contacts.
Day 2: Identify 5 new professionals you want to connect with.
Day 3: Draft your personal elevator pitch.
Day 4: Practice your pitch aloud or record yourself.
Day 5: Review your LinkedIn profile and ensure your headline reflects your expertise.
Day 6: Optimise your LinkedIn summary and key skills.
Day 7: Reflect on Week 1. Refine your pitch and LinkedIn profile.

Week 2: Reaching Out & Engaging

Day 8: Send 2-3 personalised connection requests.
Day 9: Comment thoughtfully on 2-3 posts in your industry.
Day 10: Share one article or insight on LinkedIn.
Day 11: Send a personalised message to a mentor or peer for advice.
Day 12: Research one upcoming networking event.
Day 13: Prepare 2-3 questions to ask during networking conversations.
Day 14: Reflect on Week 2. Note which connections were most engaging.

Week 3: Attending & Following Up

Day 15: Attend a networking event or webinar.

Day 16: Send follow-up messages to people you met at events.
Day 17: Reach out to one new professional in your field.
Day 18: Share a helpful resource with a contact.
Day 19: Comment on at least 3 posts by industry leaders.
Day 20: Practice your elevator pitch in a real conversation.
Day 21: Reflect on Week 3. Journal which strategies worked best.

Week 4: Strengthening Relationships & Offering Value

Day 22: Offer to introduce two contacts who could benefit from each other.
Day 23: Share a success story or tip on LinkedIn.
Day 24: Schedule an informational call with a professional.
Day 25: Send a thank-you note to someone who recently helped.
Day 26: Engage in a discussion in an industry group or forum.
Day 27: Identify a skill you can offer to help someone in your network.
Day 28: Review all new connections and organise them.
Day 29: Reflect on progress made in building your network.
Day 30: Celebrate your achievements and set networking goals for next month.

Conclusion: Celebrating Your Success

Action: Celebrate the connections you've made, the value you've added, and the growth you've experienced in your networking journey. Networking is an ongoing process, and by reflecting on your progress, you can refine your strategy for even greater success in the future.

What are you most proud of this month in terms of networking?

What's your next goal for networking in the coming month?

Chapter 5: Mastering the Job Application Process

Tailoring Your Application

In the competitive landscape of job searching, tailoring your application is crucial to stand out. This means taking the time to customise your resume and cover letter for each position you apply for. Generic applications often get lost in the shuffle, while a well-crafted, personalised approach demonstrates your genuine interest in the role and showcases your relevant skills effectively.

Start by carefully reading the job description and identifying the key skills and experiences the employer is seeking. Highlight these in your application, weaving them into your narrative to illustrate how your background aligns with the company's needs. For technical experts, this could mean emphasising experience in technological growth strategies and for medical professionals, this could mean managing disease of modern times, thus making a direct connection to the role you aspire to.

Moreover, consider the organisational culture and values of the company. Research their mission statement and recent projects to gain insights into their priorities. Reflect this understanding in your application by using language that resonates with their ethos. For instance, if applying to a company that values mindfulness, incorporating that concept into your narrative can set you apart from other candidates.

Don't forget the power of storytelling in your application. Share specific examples that demonstrate your success in previous roles, especially those that relate directly to the position. For coaches, recounting a transformative experience with a client can illustrate your capability and approach, making your application memorable and impactful.

Finally, always proofread your application meticulously. Spelling and grammatical errors can undermine your professionalism and attention to detail. A polished application not only reflects well on you but also shows respect for the potential employer. Tailoring your application is more than just a strategy; it is a way to present your authentic self in a competitive job market, particularly for the diverse coaching niches you may be targeting.

Writing Compelling Cover Letters

Crafting a compelling cover letter is an essential skill for job seekers, particularly those who are applying for roles which they are not introduced to or are applying online on job search platforms. A well-structured cover letter serves as an introduction and a marketing tool that highlights your unique qualifications, experiences, and the value you can bring to a potential employer. It is not merely a summary of your CV; rather, it is an opportunity to convey your personality and passion for the role, making it clear why you are the ideal candidate.

To begin with, personalisation is key. Addressing the cover letter to a specific person rather than using generic salutations can make a significant difference. Researching the company and the hiring manager demonstrates your interest in the position and helps you tailor your message.

Furthermore, sharing a brief anecdote related to the niche you specialise in can establish a connection and illustrate your understanding of the industry.

Utilising action-oriented language is another effective strategy. Instead of stating responsibilities, showcase your achievements and the impact you've made in previous roles. For instance, if you are an executive manager or a leader, you might emphasise how your management methods helped team-members improve their productivity and how your strategies took a client or business to the next level.

This not only highlights your expertise but also aligns your experiences with the needs of the employer.

Moreover, integrating specific keywords related to your niche can enhance the visibility of your cover letter. Usingterms that resonate with the values and objectives of the organisation you are applying to can create a powerful alignment. For example, if you are applying for a wellness and health coaching position, mention concepts such as holistic health, client-centred approaches, or evidence based strategies to resonate with the employer's mission.

Lastly, conclude your cover letter with a strong closing statement that expresses enthusiasm for the role and a desire for further discussion. This final impression can leave a lasting impact, encouraging the hiring manager to consider you for an interview.By following these strategies, job seekers, can create compelling cover letters that effectively communicate their potential
and fit for the role.

Following Up After Applications

Following up after submitting job applications is a crucial step in the job search process that many candidates overlook. It demonstrates your enthusiasm and commitment to the position, setting you apart from other applicants. By reaching out, you not only express your continued interest but also remind the hiring manager of your qualifications, which can make a significant difference in a competitive job market.

When crafting your follow-up communication, it's important to be professional and concise. A brief email or phone call can suffice, where you thank the employer for the opportunity to apply and inquire about the status of your application. This approach shows that you are proactive and engaged, qualities that employers value in potential employees. Make sure to personalise your message, referencing specific aspects of the job or interview that resonated with you.

Timing is also essential when following up. Generally, waiting about one to two weeks after submitting your application is advisable, as this gives the hiring team adequate time to review candidates. However, if you were given a timeline during the interview process, respect that period and follow up after it has passed. This strategic timing can showcase your patience and respect for the employer's process while still keeping you on their radar.

Moreover, consider how your follow-up can align with your overall personal branding. As an expert in your industry, you understand the importance of consistency in messaging. Use this opportunity to reinforce your unique value proposition and the skills you bring to the table.

Mention any relevant accomplishments or experiences that align with the job, and don't hesitate to share additional insights or materials that may support your application.

Finally, always be prepared for any outcome following your follow-up. Whether you receive good news or constructive feedback, approach the situation with a positive mindset. Each interaction is a chance to grow and refine your approach, and even a rejection can provide invaluable lessons for future applications.

Remember, persistence and resilience are key components of a successful job search, and following up is an integral part of that journey.

1 .Mastering the Job Application process: Practical Steps

Step 1: Tailor Your Resume

Action: Review each job description and customise your resume to highlight the skills, achievements, and experiences most relevant to that role.

Example: For a client/customer facing role emphasise client outcomes and satisfaction. For sales role, highlight what was the company's sale previously and what it is now after you join the company.

Tool/Goal: Use a spreadsheet to track which version of your resume you used for each application.

Step 2: Craft a Compelling Cover Letter

Action: Write a cover letter personalised for each application. Include a brief anecdote, highlight key achievements, and reflect the company's values.

Example: "I recently helped a client reduce stress by 40% through a personalised mindfulness program, and I am excited to bring similar strategies to your wellness team:'
Tool/Goal: Maintain a template that can be customised quickly for each application.

Step 3: Optimise Your Online Profiles

Action: Ensure Linkedln and other relevant platforms match your tailored resume and showcase your expertise.

Example: Update your Linked In headline: "Eye Surgeon" I Helping patients see the world clearly and live their best lives I Eye Specialist, Optometry Professional:"

Tool/Goal: Spend 30-60 minutes per week reviewing and updating your profiles.

Step 4: Apply Strategically

Action: Focus on roles that align with your skills and career goals, rather than mass-applying.

Example: Apply to 3-5 positions per week that closely match your niche.

Tool/Goal: Keep a tracker of all applications, including job title, company, date applied, and status.

Step 5: Follow Up on Applications

Action: Send a concise, professional follow-up 1-2 weeks after submission. Reiterate your interest and highlight key skills.

Example: "Hello [Hiring Manager], I wanted to follow up on my application for [Role]. I'm excited about the opportunity to bring my expertise in [Skill/Area] to your team:"

Tool/Goal: Schedule reminders to follow up and track responses in your application tracker.

Step 6: Reflect and Improve

Action: Review feedback and outcomes from applications to refine your resume, cover letter, and approach.

Example: If an application didn't get a response, adjust your cover letter to better match the job requirements.

Tool/Goal: Keep a journal of lessons learned to improve future applications.

2. Putting It All Together: A 30-Day Job Application Mastery plan

Week 1: Resume & Cover Letter Preparation

Day 1: Choose 2 job listings and read them thoroughly.
Day 2: Highlight key skills and responsibilities for each job.
Day 3: Tailor your Cover Letter and CV for Job 1and Job 2.

Day 4: Obtain feedback from peers on CV and cover letters.
Day 5: Find the hiring manager or decision maker from the prospect company.
Day 6: Draft a personalised message to arrange informational interview.
Day 7: Proofread and finalise CVs and Cover Letters.

Week 2: Optimising Online Presence

Day 8: Review Linked In profile; update headline and summary.
Day 9: Add relevant skills, certifications, or achievements.
Day 10: Share an insightful post or article related to your field.
Day 11: Engage with 2-3 posts by industry leaders.
Day 12: Join one relevant Linked In or Facebook group.
Day 13: Update any other professional online profiles (portfolio, website).
Day 14: Reflect on your online presence and refine your content.

Week 3: Applying Strategically

Day 15: Submit 3 tailored applications.
Day 16: Engage with the prospect employers and identify hiring managers.
Day 17: Track all applications in a spreadsheet (company, role, date).
Day 18: Research 2 companies you want to apply to next.
Day 19: Tailor your CV and Cover letter for Company 1and Company 2.
Day 20: Submit application and seek feedback on all applications.
Day 21: Follow up and reflect on the week.

Week 4: Following Up & Continuous Improvement

Day 22: Follow up on applications submitted 1-2 weeks ago.
Day 23: Send personalised thank-you notes to anyone who gave advice or insight.
Day 24: Review feedback or responses received and identify improvements.
Day 25: Tailor and submit another application to a targeted company.
Day 26: Follow up on networking contacts relevant to job applications.
Day 27: Journal lessons learned and update templates for CVs/cover letters.
Day 28: Share an article or post showcasing your expertise on Linked In.
Day 29: Apply to at least 2 more roles using refined templates.
Day 30: Celebrate progress and set goals for the next month of applications.

Chapter 5: Mastering the Job Application Process Practical Journal

This journal is designed to break down each section of Chapter 5 into actionable steps. Use it to track your progress, reflect on your application process, and make improvements as you move through the job search journey.

Step 1: Tailor Your Resume

1.1: Job Description Analysis

Action: Review the job description thoroughly and highlight key skills, experiences, and responsibilities that the employers are seeking.

What 3 main skills are most emphasised?

What experience or qualifications do they value most?

1.2: Tailor Your Resume

Action: Customise your resume to highlight these key skills and experiences. Ensure that your achievements reflect the job's requirements.

What specific achievements will you highlight to match the job description?

Is there a way to quantify your success (e.g., increased sales by X%, improved team productivity by X%)?

1.3: Reflection

What challenges did you face in tailoring your resume?

Were there any gaps in your experience that you wish you could address?

How can you overcome these gaps in future applications?

Progress Tracker:

Date Applied:
Job Title:
Company:
Version of CV Used:

Step 2: Craft a Compelling Cover Letter

2.1: Personalisation & Research

Action: Research the company to understand its mission, culture, and values. Find out who the hiring manager is and address them directly.

How did the company's values align with your own?

Who did you address the letter to and why?

2.2: Storytelling

Action: Use a brief anecdote to demonstrate how you've succeeded in similar situations or roles.

What personal experience or achievement connects directly to this job?

How can you tie your strengths to the company's needs?

2.3: Reflection

How confident are you in the impact of your cover letter?

Did you feel like you captured the essence of the job and your qualifications in the letter?

Progress Tracker:

Date Applied:
Job Title:
Company:
Version of Cover Letter and CV Used:

Step 3: Optimise Your Online Presence

3.1: LinkedIn Profile Update

Action: Review your LinkedIn profile. Update your headline, skills, and summary to align with the roles you're applying for.

Does your headline clearly convey your expertise and career focus?

Have you added any recent achievements or certifications?

3.2: Engagement

Action: Engage with posts from industry leaders, join relevant groups, or share an article that reflects your expertise.

What posts did you engage with?

Did you notice any new connections or comments on your profile?

3.3: Reflection

How does your LinkedIn profile compare to the job roles you're applying for?

Did your updates improve your visibility or engagement?

Progress Tracker:

Profile Updates Made (List):
Engagement (Post/Article/Comment):
Connections Gained:

Step 4: Apply Strategically

4.1: Job Selection

Action: Focus on applying to roles that align with your skills and career goals.

How did you select the jobs you applied for this week?

Do these roles align with your long-term career path?

4.2: Application Tracker

Action: Use a tracker to log every job application you submit.

Which applications are you most excited about and why?

What gaps in your experience did you notice during this process?

4.3: Reflection

What was the most challenging part of applying?

How will you approach your next set of applications differently?

Progress Tracker:

Job Applied to:
Date Submitted:
Company:
Status (Pending, Interview, Rejected):

Step 5: Follow Up on Applications

5.1: Follow-Up Timing

Action: Set a reminder to follow up 1-2 weeks after submitting your application.

Did you personalise your follow-up email?

How confident are you in your message?

5.2: Follow-Up Reflection

Action: Reflect on the follow-up process and how it feels.

What responses did you receive?

Did following up boost your confidence or create additional opportunities?

Progress Tracker:

Job Title:
Company:

Follow-Up Date:
Response:

Step 6: Reflect and Improve

6.1: Feedback Review

Action: After each job application process (whether successful or not), reflect on feedback and outcomes.

What feedback did you receive from employers, peers, or mentors?

What did you learn that you can apply in the next application cycle?

6.2: Continuous Improvement

Action: Use feedback to make continuous improvements to your resume, cover letter, or interview skills.

What improvements will you make to your application materials for next time?

Progress Tracker:

Job Title:
Company:
Feedback Received:
Action Taken for Improvement:

30-Day Job Application Plan Tracker

Each day, track your actions, reflect, and set the goal for the following day. At the end of the week, review your progress and adjust where necessary.

Week	Day	Action	Notes/Reflections
Week 1	Day 1-3	Tailor Resume & Cover Letter	
Week 1	Day 4-7	Get Feedback & Finalize	
Week 2	Day 8-10	Optimize LinkedIn & Online Presence	
Week 2	Day 11-14	Engage with Industry Leaders	
Week 3	Day 15-17	Submit Applications	
Week 3	Day 18-21	Track & Follow Up	
Week 4	Day 22-24	Reflect on Feedback	
Week 4	Day 25-30	Apply to New Jobs, Adjust Approach	

CHAPTER 6:
ACING THE INTERVIEW

Preparing for Common Interview Questions

Preparing for common interview questions is a crucial step in the job search process. Job seekers must anticipate the types of questions they will face and develop thoughtful responses. This preparation not only boosts confidence but also enables candidates to present themselves effectively. By understanding the purpose behind these questions, candidates can tailor their answers to highlight their unique skills and experiences.

One of the most frequently asked questions is, "Tell me about yourself." This question allows candidates to share their professional journey in a concise manner. It is essential to structure this response by focusing on relevant experiences that align with the job being applied for. Candidates should aim to create a narrative that connects their past roles to the potential contributions they can make in the new position.

Behavioural questions are another common aspect of interviews, often starting with phrases like, "Can you give me an example of...?" These questions assess how candidates handle specific situations in the workplace. Job seekers should prepare by reflecting on their past experiences and identifying key examples that demonstrate their problem-solving skills, teamwork, and adaptability. Practicing these scenarios can help candidates articulate their thoughts clearly during the interview.

Additionally, candidates should be prepared for questions regarding their strengths and weaknesses. This is an opportunity to showcase self-awareness and personal growth. When discussing strengths, candidates should align them with the job requirements, while for weaknesses, it's important to highlight steps taken to improve. This approach not only displays honesty but also a commitment to professional development.

Lastly, candidates should not overlook the importance of asking questions during the interview. This demonstrates genuine interest in the role and the company. Questions can range from inquiries about company culture to specifics about team dynamics. By preparing thoughtful questions, candidates can leave a lasting impression and further establish their suitability for the position.

Body Language and Presentation Skills

In the realm of job searching, body language plays an integral role in how individuals are perceived during interviews and networking events. Non-verbal cues, such as posture, gestures, and facial expressions, can significantly impact the impression you make on potential employers. Understanding these elements can empower job seekers to convey confidence and professionalism, essential traits that hiring managers look for in candidates. By mastering body language, you can enhance your overall presentation skills, making you a more compelling choice for any position.

Effective body language begins with posture. Standing or sitting up straight not only conveys confidence but also helps to project authority and competence.

Slouching or appearing overly relaxed can send the message that you lack enthusiasm or seriousness about the opportunity at hand. Additionally, open body language, such as uncrossed arms and a relaxed stance, invites engagement and fosters a positive connection with your audience. These subtle changes can make a significant difference in how you are perceived during crucial interactions.

Gestures also play a pivotal role in communication. Using appropriate hand movements can help emphasise key points and keep the listener's attention. However, excessive or distracting gestures can detract from your message and create a sense of nervousness. Striking the right balance is essential; practice your gestures in front of a mirror or record yourself to evaluate which movements enhance your presentation and which may hinder it. This self-awareness will help you refine your delivery and make a lasting impression.

Facial expressions are another vital aspect of body language that can communicate enthusiasm and sincerity. A warm smile can go a long way in creating a positive atmosphere during interviews, while maintaining eye contact demonstrates attentiveness and confidence. Be mindful of your expressions, as they should align with the message you are conveying. Practicing in front of a friend or mentor can provide valuable feedback on your facial expressions, ensuring they enhance rather than detract from your overall presentation.

Ultimately, mastering body language and presentation skills is about being authentic and engaging. It is essential for job seekers to align their non-verbal cues with their verbal communication to create a cohesive and persuasive narrative.

As you prepare for your job search, consider how you can incorporate these techniques into your approach. By doing so, you will not only boost your confidence but also significantly increase your chances of making a positive impression on potential employers.

Handling Difficult Interview Situations

Navigating difficult interview situations can be a daunting task for job seekers, particularly when faced with challenging questions or unexpected scenarios. It's essential to approach these situations with a calm and collected mindset. Practice mindfulness techniques that can help guide your thoughts and reduce anxiety before and during an interview. Remember, how you react in these moments can demonstrate your ability to handle pressure, a trait many employers value highly.

One common difficult situation is when an interviewer asks a question that catches you off guard. Instead of panicking, take a deep breath and allow yourself a moment to think. It's perfectly acceptable to pause and gather your thoughts. You can also request to rephrase the question to buy yourself time and ensure you understand what is being asked. This not only shows your confidence but also your ability to communicate effectively under stress.

Another challenging scenario may arise if the interviewer seems to be unfriendly or dismissive. In such cases, it is vital to remain professional and composed. Responding with grace can turn the situation around and potentially build rapport. Demonstrating emotional intelligence, a skill often emphasised in industries like police, government agencies, cyber security, etc. can help you navigate these interpersonal dynamics, allowing you to maintain your confidence and self-esteem throughout the interview.

Additionally, consider preparing for difficult questions ahead of time. This preparation can include reflecting on your past experiences, both positive and negative, and thinking about how they have shaped your professional journey.By proactively addressing your weaknesses or failures, you will be better equipped to answer tough questions honestly and constructively, showcasing your growth mindset.

Lastly, remember that every interview is a two-way street. If the environment feels uncomfortable or the questions seem inappropriate, trust your instincts. You have the right to assess whether this role and organisation align with your values and goals. A strong sense of self-awareness, which is often developed through coaching, positive self-talks, and consciousness will empower you to make informed decisions about your career path, even in challenging situations.

1. Acing the Interview: Practical Steps

Step 1: Prepare for Common Interview Questions

Action: Identify frequently asked questions and craft thoughtful, relevant responses.

Example: For "Tell me about yourself:' structure your answer to highlight experiences that match the role.

Tool/Goal: Create a list of 10-15 common questions and write down concise, compelling answers for each.

Step 2: Prepare Behavioural Examples

Action: Reflect on past experiences to answer, "Can you give me an example of...?"

Example: For "Tell me about yourself:' structure your answer to highlight experiences that match the role.

Examples:
"When leading a project (Situation), I noticed engagement was low (Task). I implemented interactive exercises (Action), resulting in 95% positive feedback from project participants (Result):'

"When training a new sales team (Situation), I found that they were struggling to meet their quarterly quotas (Task). I created a mentorship program that paired junior and senior team members and conducted bi weekly role-playing sessions (Action), which resulted in the team exceeding their quota by 15% in the following quarter (Result)."

Situation: The company's network was slow and unreliable. Task: Identify and fix the root cause of frequent outages. Action: I audited the network, found a misconfigured server, and migrated services to a new, optimised environment. Result: Network uptime increased to 99.9% and support tickets were reduced by 15%.

Tool/Goal: Prepare at least 5 STAR examples covering teamwork, problem solving, leadership, and adaptability.

Step 3: Highlight Strengths and Address Weaknesses

Action: Identify your top strengths and areas for growth, linking them to the job.

Example:

Strength: "Strong communication skills to understand client's needs"
Weakness: "Initially struggled with time management; now use digital tools, journaling, and appropriate calendars to stay organised"

Tool/Goal: Keep a short reference sheet for self-awareness points to revisit before interviews.

Step 4: Practice Body Language & Presentation

Action: Work on posture, gestures, facial expressions, and eye contact to convey confidence.

Example: Sit up straight, smile naturally, and use hand gestures to emphasise
key points.

Tool/Goal: Record a mock interview or practise in front of a friend/mentor to refine presentation skills.

Step 5: Handle Difficult Questions & Situations

Action: Prepare strategies for challenging scenarios, including unexpected or tricky questions.

Example: Pause, take a breath, rephrase the question if needed, and answer honestly with a growth-oriented perspective.

Tool/Goal: List potential difficult questions (e.g., gaps in employment, handling conflicts) and draft calm, professional responses.

Step 6: Ask Thoughtful Questions
Action: Prepare 3-5 insightful questions to ask the interviewer.

Example:
- "Can you describe the team culture?"
- "What professional development opportunities are available?"

Tool/Goal: Use these questions to demonstrate engagement and genuine interest.

Step 7: Follow-Up After Interviews

Action: Send a personalised thank-you email within 24-48 hours.

Example:
"Thank you for your time today. I enjoyed learning about your team and am excited about the opportunity to contribute my industry experience:'
"Thank you for your time today. I truly enjoyed learning more about the company's vision and how my experience in project management can help you achieve your goals."
"Thank you for your time today. It was great to hear about the company culture, and I'm very excited about the chance to grow with your team and take the organisation to the next level."

Tool/Goal: Maintain a tracker of interviews and follow-ups to ensure timely communication.

Step 8: Reflect and Improve

Action: After each interview, evaluate your performance and identify areas for improvement.

Example: Note which questions were challenging, how well your body language conveyed confidence, and lessons learned.

Tool/Goal: Keep a journal for continuous refinement and growth for future interviews.

2. Putting It All Together: A 30-Day Interview acing plan

Week 1: Common Questions & Self-Awareness

Day 1: List 10-15 common interview questions.
Day 2: Draft answers for "Tell me about yourself' and key personal strengths.
Day 3: Prepare responses for weaknesses or gaps.
Day 4: Identify 5 behavioural examples using the STAR method.
Day 5: Practice answers aloud.
Day 6: Record yourself answering 3-5 questions; review for clarity.
Day 7: Journal reflections and refine responses.

Week 2: Body Language & Presentation

Day 8: Practise posture and eye contact in front of a mirror.
Day 9: Work on appropriate hand gestures to emphasise points.
Day 10: Practice smiling naturally and showing enthusiasm.

Day 11: Record a full mock interview; assess body language and tone.
Day 12: Ask a friend/mentor to critique presentation skills.
Day 13: Adjust based on feedback; focus on non-verbal cues.
Day 14: Reflect on progress and journal improvements.

Week 3: Difficult Questions & Scenarios

Day 15: List potential tricky questions for your niche.
Day 16: Draft calm, professional responses for each.
Day 17: Practice rephrasing and pausing before answering challenging questions.
Day 18: Role-play a mock interview with a friend handling unexpected scenarios.
Day 19: Reflect on emotional responses and identify strategies to stay composed.
Day 20: Refine answers and prepare fallback examples for difficult questions.
Day 21: Journal lessons learned and track confidence improvements.

Week 4: Final Preparation & Follow-Up

Day 22: Prepare 3-5 thoughtful questions to ask interviewers.
Day 23: Conduct a full mock interview incorporating body language, STAR examples, and questions.
Day 24: Review your online presence and ensure it aligns with interview messaging.
Day 25: Draft thank-you email templates for follow-ups.
Day 26: Send a follow-up email for any recent interviews.
Day 27: Review feedback from mock interviews; refine responses further.

Day 28: Practice mindfulness or relaxation techniques to reduce interview anxiety.
Day 29: Review all STAR examples, questions, and key points.
Day 30: Celebrate progress and set goals for upcoming interviews.

Chapter 6:
Interview Preparation Journal & Progress Tracker

This journal is designed to help you develop and refine your approach to job interviews, combining **actionable tasks** with **insightful reflections** that track your progress.

Section 1: Common Interview Questions & Self-Awareness

Action:

1. List your top 10-15 common interview questions. Start with general questions such as:

"Tell me about yourself."

"Why should we hire you?"

"Where do you see yourself in 5 years?"

"Where do you see yourself in 5 years?"

Tailor the list to your specific field (e.g., "How do you handle security breaches?" for cybersecurity roles).

Reflection Prompts:

How do you feel when answering each question?

Which questions are you prepared for and which make you uncomfortable?

What parts of your background need further clarity for each question?

Section 2: Crafting Your Story & STAR Method Action:

2. **Prepare 3-5 behavioral examples using the STAR method (Situation, Task, Action, Result).**

Situation: What was the challenge?

Task: What was your responsibility?

Action: What steps did you take?

Result: What was the outcome?
Example:

"When managing a cross-functional team (Situation), we were tasked with launching a product in 3 months (Task).

I facilitated weekly meetings and streamlined communication (Action), leading to a successful launch ahead of schedule (Result)."

Reflection Prompts:

Do your examples align with the qualities the employer is looking for?

Are there specific examples that can be strengthened or clarified?

Which examples do you feel most confident in presenting during the interview?

Section 3: Strengths and Weaknesses
Action:

3. **Identify 2-3 of your key strengths and weaknesses.**

Strengths: Choose strengths that align directly with the job you're applying for (e.g., problem-solving, leadership, technical skills).

Weaknesses: Select areas where you've shown growth or are actively improving. Prepare a plan of action to demonstrate how you're addressing these weaknesses (e.g., "I used to struggle with time management but now use digital tools to prioritise tasks").

Reflection Prompts:

Do your strengths reflect what the employer is seeking in the role?

How comfortable are you discussing your weaknesses?

Have you seen significant improvement in your weaknesses?

How will you frame your weaknesses in a way that shows growth or resilience?

Section 4: Body Language & Presentation
Action:

4. **Work on posture, hand gestures, facial expressions, and eye contact.**

Practice your body language in front of a mirror or record yourself. Focus on:

Posture: Sit or stand tall to project confidence.

Gestures: Use natural hand movements to emphasise key points.

Facial Expressions: Ensure your expressions align with your message—smiling, nodding, showing engagement.

Eye Contact: Maintain steady eye contact to show attentiveness.

Reflection Prompts:

How do you feel about your body language?

Do you feel your gestures enhance your answers or distract from them?

Are there any habits (e.g., fidgeting, avoiding eye contact) that need to be minimised?

Section 5: Handling Difficult Situations
Action:

5. **Prepare for challenging questions or scenarios.**
For example:

Gaps in employment: Be ready to explain them positively (e.g., "I took time off to pursue further education" or "I focused on personal development during that time").

Conflict or failure: Prepare stories that focus on lessons learned and how you've grown.

Reflection Prompts:

How do you feel when answering tough or unexpected questions?

What emotions arise when discussing your weaknesses, failure, or gaps in your resume?

Do you feel calm and composed, or is there room for improvement in your response delivery?

Section 6: Asking Questions to the Interviewer
Action:

6. **Prepare a list of insightful questions to ask the interviewer.**

Example questions might include:

"Can you tell me about the company culture?"

“How does the team collaborate on projects?”

“What is the biggest challenge the team faces right now?”

"How do you support professional development within the company?”

Reflection Prompts:

Do your questions reflect genuine interest in the company and the role?

How confident are you in asking these questions?

What new information are you hoping to gain from asking these questions?

Section 7: Mock Interviews & Feedback
Action:

7. **Conduct mock interviews.**

Schedule at least 2-3 mock interviews with a friend, mentor, or colleague. Focus on:

Responding to common and difficult questions.

Practicing body language and non-verbal cues.

Asking thoughtful questions to the interviewer.
After each mock interview, ask for feedback on your responses, tone, body language, and overall impression.

Reflection Prompts:

What feedback did you receive that surprised you?

What part of the interview did you feel most confident in?

Were there any areas (e.g., specific questions, body language) that need more work?

Did you feel more comfortable and composed during the second or third mock interview?

Section 8: Final Preparation & Follow-Up Action:

8. **Prepare a personalised thank-you email** to send within 24 hours after an interview.

Example:
"Thank you for the opportunity to interview for the [role]. I enjoyed learning more about your team and the exciting challenges ahead. I'm confident that my skills in [specific skill] would contribute to the team's success. I look forward to hearing from you soon."

Reflection Prompts:

How confident are you in your follow-up communication?

Does your thank-you email reflect your genuine interest in the role?

How can you make sure your communication stays timely and professional?

Section 9: Post-Interview Reflection
Action:

9. **Reflect on each interview.**

After each interview, note down:

What went well (e.g., strong answers, engaging body language).

What could have been improved (e.g., weak answers, nervousness).

Any lessons learned from the interviewer's feedback or your own performance.

Reflection Prompts:

What were the main takeaways from the interview?

What adjustments will you make for future interviews?

How did the interview align with your expectations about the company and role?

Progress Tracker

Date	Activity Completed	Insights / Improvements	Next Steps
	Created 15 common interview questions	Identified 3 questions that make me nervous	Prepare more confident responses for nervous questions
	Practiced STAR method with 4 examples	Improved clarity in demonstrating leadership	Add more specific results to demonstrate impact
	Mock interview with a mentor	Received feedback on body language	Focus on maintaining eye contact during answers
	Follow-up email sent	Felt confident in my closing message	Prepare follow-up emails for

	after interview		next interviews
	Reflected on interview performance	Improved handling of tough questions	Practice rephrasing tough questions for future interviews

Insights / Improvements:

What skills or techniques did you improve the most? What areas do you still need to work on for next time? How has your confidence grown throughout this preparation process?

Skils or Techniques:
Areas of interest/focus:
Confidence grown:

Next Steps:

CHAPTER 7: PERSONAL FINANCE DURING JOB TRANSITION

Budgeting for Unemployment

Navigating unemployment can be a daunting experience, both emotionally and financially. It's essential to approach this period with a well-structured budget to alleviate some of the stress associated with job searching. Understanding your current financial situation is the first step. Begin by assessing your savings, expenses, and any potential income sources, such as unemployment benefits. This clarity will help you make informed decisions about how to allocate your resources effectively during this transitional phase.

Once you have a clear picture of your finances, it's time to create a budget tailored to your needs as a job seeker. Prioritising essential expenses such as housing, utilities, and food is crucial. You may need to cut back on non-essential spending, such as dining out or subscriptions, to ensure your finances remain stable. By focusing on necessities, you can extend your financial runway while you search for new employment opportunities.

In addition to managing current expenses, consider seeking additional income sources to support your budget. This could involve temporary or part-time work, freelancing, or utilising skills you possess in a different capacity. Exploring these options not only helps financially but can also provide a sense of purpose and structure during a period that may otherwise feel overwhelming. It's about being proactive and creative in your approach.

Moreover, it's important to regularly review and adjust your budget as your circumstances change. If you secure interviews or freelance work, be sure to update your financial plan accordingly. Conversely, if unexpected expenses arise, adapt your budget to accommodate these changes. Staying flexible will empower you to manage your finances effectively and reduce anxiety surrounding unemployment.

Finally, remember that budgeting during unemployment is not just about survival; it's also about preparation for your next career move. Investing in your personal development, such as coaching sessions, workshops, or courses, can enhance your skills and boost your confidence. By viewing this time as an opportunity for growth, you can emerge from unemployment not only financially stable but also professionally enriched, ready to tackle new challenges with renewed vigour.

Understanding Severance and Benefits

Understanding severance and benefits is crucial for job seekers, especially during times of transition. Severance packages are often offered by employers to employees who are laid off or terminated under specific conditions. These packages typically include financial compensation, which can provide a vital buffer while searching for new employment. It's important to understand the terms of any severance agreement, as they can vary significantly between companies and individual contracts.

In addition to financial compensation, severance packages may include continued health benefits, outplacement services, and other forms of support. Job seekers should investigate what benefits are available to them and how long they will last.

This knowledge can help individuals make informed decisions about their job search strategy and financial planning. It is essential to weigh the benefits of accepting a severance package against the potential of finding a new position quickly.

Another critical aspect of understanding severance is knowing your rights. Employees should be aware of any legal requirements that govern severance packages in their jurisdiction. This includes understanding whether a severance agreement is voluntary or if it is a condition of termination. Seeking guidance from a career coach or legal advisor can help clarify these complexities, ensuring that job seekers are fully informed.

Moreover, severance negotiations can be a pivotal moment for job seekers. Approaching these discussions with confidence and clarity can significantly affect the outcome. Those working with a coach can learn effective negotiation techniques that not only improve their severance terms but also bolster their overall confidence during the job search process. This empowerment can lead to better job offers and career satisfaction.

Finally, understanding severance and benefits extends beyond the immediate financial implications. It can impact a job seeker's mental and emotional well-being. Transitioning from one job to another can be stressful, and having a clear understanding of what to expect can alleviate some of that stress. By equipping themselves with knowledge about severance and benefits, job seekers can navigate their career changes more effectively, ultimately leading to greater success in their job search journey.

Planning for Future Financial Stability

Planning for future financial stability is crucial for job seekers who aim to create a secure and prosperous life. By setting clear financial goals, individuals can establish a roadmap that guides their decisions and actions. It's essential to assess current financial situations, including income, expenses, debts, and savings, in order to identify areas that require improvement. This thorough understanding helps to form a solid foundation for building a stable financial future. Creating a budget is a vital step in the planning process. A well-structured budget allows job seekers to allocate their resources effectively, ensuring that they live within their means while still setting aside funds for savings and investments.

Moreover, monitoring spending habits can highlight unnecessary expenditures that can be reduced or eliminated. This practice not only enhances financial awareness but also fosters a sense of control over personal finances, empowering individuals in their job search journey.

Investing in personal development is another essential aspect of financial stability. Job seekers should consider furthering their education or acquiring new skills that align with market demands. This proactive approach not only increases employability but can also lead to higher earning potential in the long run. Engaging with coaches in various niches, such as personal finance and wellness, can provide valuable insights and strategies for making informed decisions about investments in oneself.

Additionally, building an emergency fund is critical for financial security. Having a safety net can alleviate stress during the job search process and provide peace of mind when unexpected expenses arise. Experts generally recommend saving at least three to six months' worth of living expenses. This fund can serve as a buffer, allowing job seekers to focus on finding the right opportunity without the pressure of immediate financial strain.

Lastly, seeking guidance from financial professionals or coaches can enhance one's financial literacy and strategic thinking. These experts can offer tailored advice and support, helping individuals to navigate their unique circumstances effectively. By embracing a proactive approach to financial planning, job seekers can pave the way toward a more secure and fulfilling future, ultimately empowering their career pursuits.

1. Personal Finance During Job Transition:
Practical Steps

Step 1: Assess Your Current Financial Situation
Action: Review savings, monthly expenses, and potential income sources such as unemployment benefits.

Example: List all monthly bills, subscriptions, and essential expenses alongside current savings.

Tool/Goal: Use a spreadsheet or budgeting app to track finances and calculate how long savings will last.

Step 2: Create a Job Seeker Budget

Action: Prioritise essential expenses and identify areas to cut non-essential spending.

Example: Reduce dining out, pause subscriptions, and focus spending on housing, utilities, and food.

Tool/Goal: Develop a monthly budget that ensures financial stability while searching for a new role.

Step 3: Explore Additional Income Opportunities

Action: Consider temporary work, freelancing, or using transferable skills in different roles.

Example: Take on a freelance project or part-time work to supplement income.

Tool/Goal: Aim to identify at least one income-generating opportunity per week during unemployment.

Step 4: Understand Severance and Benefits

Action: Review severance agreements, legal rights, and any ongoing benefits.

Example: Check whether severance includes continued health coverage or outplacement services.

Tool/Goal: Consult a career coach or legal advisor to ensure you understand terms and can negotiate if needed.

Step 5: Regularly Review and Adjust Finances

Action: Update your budget as circumstances change, including new income or unexpected expenses.

Example: Revise spending plan after a freelance payment or interview travel expense.

Tool/Goal: Conduct weekly financial reviews to maintain control and flexibility.

Step 6: Plan for Future Financial Stability

Action: Set clear financial goals and build a roadmap to achieve them.

Example: Create a savings target, plan skill investments, and develop an emergency fund.

Tool/Goal: Allocate funds for personal development and aim to save 3-6 months' living expenses.

Step 7: Seek Professional Guidance

Action: Consult financial advisors or coaches for tailored advice.

Example: Engage with a personal finance coach to strategise savings, investments, and budgeting.

Tool/Goal: Implement recommended strategies to increase financial literacy and long-term security.

2. Putting It All Together: A 30-Day Personal Finance and job

Week 1: Assess & Plan transition plan

Day 1: List all savings, monthly expenses, and current debts.
Day 2: Calculate your monthly essential and non-essential spending.
Day 3: Research unemployment benefits or temporary income options.

Day 4: Set short-term financial priorities (e.g., rent, utilities, food).
Day 5: Identify areas to reduce discretionary spending.
Day 6: Record a baseline of your financial situation.
Day 7: Reflect on the first week and adjust your spending plan as needed.

Week 2: Budget Implementation

Day 8: Draft a detailed monthly budget based on essential expenses.
Day 9: Track spending daily using a spreadsheet or budgeting app.
Day 10: Pause unnecessary subscriptions or memberships.
Day 11: Allocate funds for potential job search-related costs (e.g., travel, CV services).
Day 12: Evaluate your discretionary spending and adjust if needed.
Day 13: Research temporary or freelance opportunities.
Day 14: Reflect on budget effectiveness and update as necessary.

Week 3: Understanding Benefits & Additional Income

Day 15: Review severance agreements or benefits packages.
Day 16: Contact a career coach or legal advisor to clarify terms.
Day 17: Identify at least one freelance or part-time work opportunity.
Day 18: Apply for temporary roles or pitch freelance services.
Day 19: Track income from new opportunities.
Day 20: Adjust budget to include additional income.

Day 21: Reflect on financial progress and note lessons learned.

Week 4: Long-Term Stability & Professional Guidance

Day 22: Set long-term financial goals (savings, emergency fund, skill investment).
Day 23: Allocate funds each week towards these goals.
Day 24: Meet with a financial advisor or coach for tailored advice.
Day 25: Review current investments and consider personal development options.
Day 26: Update your emergency fund target and savings plan.
Day 27: Track your progress and celebrate small achievements.
Day 28: Reflect on lessons learned from budgeting and income planning.
Day 29: Identify one area to further optimise finances next month.
Day 30: Review your 30-day progress and set actionable financial goals for the next month.

Chapter 7: Personal Finance During Job Transition: Actionable Steps & Progress Tracker

Navigating financial challenges during a job transition is a key part of your journey. This guide is designed to help you approach personal finance during unemployment with a clear strategy, ensuring that you can stay financially stable while focusing on finding the right job. The following steps offer practical and actionable advice to manage your finances during this transitional period. Track your progress and adjust your plan as needed to keep yourself on track.

1. Assess Your Current Financial Situation

Action Steps:

Review Your Finances: Start by evaluating your current savings, monthly expenses, and any potential income sources like unemployment benefits or severance pay.

List Essential Expenses: Prioritise essential expenses such as housing, utilities, food, and transportation. Identify areas of non-essential spending (subscriptions, dining out) that you can reduce or eliminate.

Determine How Long Your Savings Will Last: Use a budgeting tool or spreadsheet to track your monthly expenses and estimate how long your savings will sustain you.

Tracking Progress:

Savings and emergency funds:
[ ] Adequate [ ] Limited [ ] Insufficient
Essential expenses listed: [ ] Yes [ ] No
Estimate of how long savings will last: ______________________

Reflection: How clear is your financial picture? Are there any unexpected expenses or income sources that need to be factored in?

2. Create a Job Seeker Budget
Action Steps:

Prioritise Essentials: Focus your spending on what is absolutely necessary. Cut back on non-essential items like dining out, entertainment subscriptions, and luxury purchases.

Create a Monthly Budget: Set up a detailed budget to track income and expenses, ensuring that essential expenses are covered while minimising unnecessary spending.

Tracking Progress:

Monthly expenses broken down: [ ] Yes [ ] No
Non-essential spending reduced: [ ] Yes [ ] No

Reflection: Are there any areas where you can reduce spending further? How does your current spending align with your job search goals?

3. Explore Additional Income Opportunities

Action Steps:

Consider Temporary or Freelance Work: Look into part-time work, freelancing, or gig economy jobs to generate additional income. Explore opportunities that align with your skills and schedule.

Leverage Transferable Skills: If you have expertise in areas such as writing, design, tutoring, or consulting, use these skills to find freelance work or short-term projects.

Tracking Progress:
Freelance or temporary opportunities explored:
[ ] 1-2 [ ] 3-4 [ ] 5+
Additional income generated: [ ] Yes [ ] No

Reflection: How has pursuing additional income helped your financial situation? Does it provide a sense of stability or purpose during your job search?

4. Understand Severance and Benefits

Action Steps:

Review Severance Package: If applicable, carefully review the terms of any severance package or unemployment benefits you're entitled to. Understand the length of time you can receive payments, any health benefits, or outplacement services.

Know Your Rights: Research the legal requirements surrounding severance and unemployment benefits in your jurisdiction. If necessary, consult a career coach or legal advisor to clarify terms.

Tracking Progress:

Severance benefits reviewed: [ ] Yes [ ] No
Legal advice or consultation sought: [ ] Yes [ ] No

Reflection: How well do you understand your severance or benefits? Have these resources affected your job search strategy or timeline?

5. Regularly Review and Adjust Finances

Action Steps:

Update Your Budget: Revisit your budget regularly to reflect any changes in income, such as freelance payments or interview-related expenses (e.g., travel).

Track Unexpected Expenses: If new costs arise (e.g., medical bills, car repair), adjust your budget accordingly to stay on track.

Tracking Progress:

Weekly budget review: [ ] Yes [ ] No
Unexpected expenses tracked: [ ] Yes [ ] No
Reflection: How easy is it to keep track of your spending? Have any new financial challenges or opportunities appeared?

6. Plan for Future Financial Stability

Action Steps:

Set Financial Goals: Develop long-term financial goals, including building an emergency fund, saving for retirement, and investing in personal development (such as courses, certifications, or coaching).

Create an Emergency Fund: Set aside funds to cover 3-6 months of living expenses. This will act as a safety net if your job search takes longer than expected.

Allocate Funds for Personal Growth: Dedicate a portion of your budget to improving your skills or pursuing educational opportunities that align with your career goals.

Tracking Progress:

Emergency fund target:

[ ] 1-2 months [ ] 3-6 months [ ] 6+ months

Personal development fund allocated: [ ] Yes [ ] No
Reflection: How do you feel about your financial future? Are your financial goals aligned with your job search priorities?

7. Seek Professional Guidance

Action Steps:

Consult a Financial Advisor: Engage with a financial expert or coach to help navigate your finances, optimise your budget, and identify investment opportunities.

Review Your Investment Strategy: If applicable, evaluate your current investments and savings strategy, ensuring that they align with your long-term goals.

Tracking Progress:

Financial advice sought: [ ] Yes [ ] No

Investment strategy reviewed: [ ] Yes [ ] No
Reflection: How has seeking financial advice impacted your financial outlook? Do you feel more confident in managing your finances moving forward?

Putting It All Together: Personal Finance & Job Search Plan

Week 1: Assess Your Current Financial Situation
List your savings, monthly expenses, and debts.
Review your unemployment benefits and any potential income sources.

Identify your financial priorities and begin adjusting your spending plan accordingly.

Week 2: Create and Implement Your Job Seeker Budget

Draft a detailed budget based on essential expenses.
Track your spending daily and identify areas to cut back.

Research temporary income opportunities and explore freelance work.

Week 3: Review Severance, Benefits, and Additional Income

Review your severance package or benefits in detail.
Seek professional advice on your severance and unemployment rights.
Identify at least one freelance or part-time job opportunity.
Adjust your budget based on new income sources.

Week 4: Long-Term Stability and Professional Guidance

Set long-term financial goals such as building an emergency fund and investing in personal development.
Meet with a financial advisor or coach to strategise for long-term financial stability.
Review and track your progress, celebrating milestones and adjusting goals as necessary.

Final Reflection:

Financial Clarity: How clear is your financial picture now compared to the start of your job search?

Financial Security: Do you feel financially secure during your transition? What steps can you take to enhance this security?

Financial Insecurity: What steps can you take to overcome the insecurity?

Plans Moving Forward: What are your top financial goals for the next month? How will they support both your job search and long-term financial stability?

If you're starting your job search from a place where you have zero money, it's essential to approach the situation with urgency and a clear set of actionable steps. The key here is to balance short-term financial survival with long-term career strategy. Here's a practical, step-by-step guide that you can apply from **Day 1** to help you regain control over your finances, while aggressively moving forward with your job search.

1. Immediate Financial Survival: What to Do Now

Step 1: Assess Your Essential Expenses

Action: Identify the absolute essentials: food, shelter (rent/mortgage), utilities, transportation, and healthcare.

How to Apply: Use a simple budgeting tool (Google Sheets, Excel, or a free app like Mint) to list all essential bills. Prioritise rent/mortgage and utilities to prevent any service interruptions.

Quick Win: Negotiate Bills: Call your landlord, utility companies, and other service providers to explain your situation and ask for extensions or reduced payments. Many providers offer hardship programs.

Step 2: Cut Unnecessary Expenses Immediately

Action: Eliminate all non-essential expenses like subscriptions (Netflix, gym, premium apps), dining out, or impulse buys.

List items that you can eliminate now:

How to Apply: Go through your bank statements and cancel any recurring payments for services you don't need right now. Cut back on discretionary spending—everything you can eliminate will give you more breathing room.

Quick Win: Pause or Downgrade Subscriptions: If you have services like streaming platforms or memberships, downgrade or pause them until you have stable income.

Step 3: Access Emergency Funds

Action: If you have any savings or assets that can be liquidated (e.g., a high-yield savings account, investment accounts), now is the time to tap into them. If you don't, consider other options.

How to Apply: Transfer funds from savings into your checking account to cover basic living expenses. If you have assets like jewellery, tech, or extra electronics, consider selling them through platforms like eBay, Facebook Marketplace, or Craigslist.

List items that you can sell:

Quick Win: Sell Unused Items: Look around your home for things you no longer need. This can give you immediate cash flow.

2. Generate Immediate Income

Step 4: Apply for Unemployment Benefits or Government Assistance

Action: Check if you're eligible for unemployment benefits, government support programs, or food assistance.

How to Apply: Visit your local government website or use platforms like **UI (Unemployment Insurance)** to apply. Even if you're unsure, it's worth exploring all possible aid during this transition.

Quick Win: Food Assistance: Apply for food stamps (SNAP) or food banks in your area if you're struggling to put food on the table.

Step 5: Explore Gig Work, Freelance, or Part-Time Opportunities

Action: Immediately start looking for flexible, low-barrier income opportunities to cover short-term expenses while you continue job hunting.

How to Apply: Sign up for gig platforms like **Uber, DoorDash, or Instacart** (for delivery) or **TaskRabbit** (for small tasks and errands). You can also explore freelance work on platforms like **Upwork, Fiverr**, or **Freelancer** for short-term projects in writing, graphic design, customer service, tutoring, or virtual assistance.

Quick Win: Freelancing or Gig Work: Register on multiple gig economy platforms and set a daily goal to earn a certain amount of money.

What can you do now to go for Gig Work or Freelancing?

Step 6: Look for Short-Term, Low-Cost Jobs

Action: Find jobs that don't require significant investment (e.g., driving, retail, delivery, temporary work).

How to Apply: Search job boards like Indeed, Glassdoor, or FlexJobs for temporary, freelance, or low-barrier positions. Look for positions that can provide immediate pay, even if they're not related to your long-term career.

Quick Win: Apply to Temp Agencies: Register with temp agencies in your area. They can sometimes provide immediate work.

3. Job Search Strategy & Networking: What to Do Now

Step 7: Update Your Resume and LinkedIn Profile

Action: Refresh your resume and LinkedIn profile with your most recent experience, highlighting transferable skills.

How to Apply: Use free templates (Google Docs, Canva) to create a clean and modern resume. Update your LinkedIn profile to reflect your job search and allow potential employers to find you. Make sure your skills and work experience are front and center.

Quick Win: Use Free Resources: There are free resume and LinkedIn profile optimisation tools such as **Resumake**, **Zety**, or **Canva** to help you get started quickly.

Step 8: Apply Aggressively

Action: Apply to **at least 5-10 jobs every day**. Tailor each application and cover letter for the specific role.

How to Apply: Use job boards like **Indeed**, **LinkedIn**, or **Glassdoor** to apply for positions that match your skills. Keep a tracker of your applications to ensure follow-ups.

Quick Win: Set a Daily Application Goal: Commit to applying to 5-10 jobs each day. Even if you're applying to lower-paying or temporary jobs, it keeps you in the rhythm and builds momentum.

Step 9: Network—Reach Out to Your Circle

Action: Tap into your personal and professional network. Let friends, family, and former colleagues know that you're actively looking for a job. Networking can often lead to hidden opportunities.

How to Apply: Send a LinkedIn message or email to people you know, asking for advice, job leads, or referrals. Don't hesitate to ask about temporary work or freelance opportunities.

Quick Win: Leverage LinkedIn: Message at least 5 people in your network every day asking for advice or job leads. Mention you are actively looking for work and specify the type of job you're targeting.

4. Focus on Your Mental and Emotional Well-Being

Step 10: Keep a Positive, Growth-Oriented Mindset

Action: Job hunting can be stressful, but it's important to stay focused on the end goal. Take time each day to engage in activities that help reduce stress and boost motivation.

How to Apply: Practice mindfulness, take walks, engage in light exercise, or meditate. Create a morning routine that sets a positive tone for your day.

Quick Win: Morning Routine: Spend 10-15 minutes each morning doing something that grounds you, whether it's a short workout, breathing exercises, or reading an inspiring book or article.

Step 11: Learn and Upskill

Action: Use any downtime to build skills that can make you more marketable.

How to Apply: There are free online courses available on platforms like **Coursera**, **edX**, and **LinkedIn Learning**. Focus on skills that are in high demand (e.g., digital marketing, data analysis, coding, project management).
Quick Win: Complete a Free Online Course: Choose one free course to complete within a week that enhances your resume and employability.

5. Long-Term Financial Strategy (When Possible)

Step 12: Build an Emergency Fund (Long-Term Focus)

Action: Once you secure some income, begin building an emergency fund to give you more financial security.

How to Apply: Aim to save at least 3-6 months' worth of expenses in a separate account for unforeseen events. Allocate a percentage of any future income towards this fund.

Quick Win: Set Up a Separate Savings Account: Open an emergency fund account and commit to saving a small percentage of any income, even if it's just 5-10% in the beginning.

Immediate Action Steps:

1. List all of your **essential bills** (rent, utilities, groceries, etc.).
2. Track your **savings** (if any) and calculate how long they'll last.
3. Use a free budgeting tool like **Mint** or a simple **spreadsheet** to track your money.
4. Cancel **subscriptions** you don't need (Netflix, gym, etc.).
5. **Stop eating out** or ordering takeout. Stick to a **basic food plan**.
6. Pause any **luxury purchases** or impulse buys until you're stable.
7. Go online and apply for unemployment benefits if eligible.
8. Look for **local programs** that offer food assistance (SNAP, food banks) and apply.
9. **Sign up for gig apps** like **Uber**, **DoorDash**, **TaskRabbit**, or **Fiverr** to start earning cash quickly.
10. If you have a specific skill (writing, design, social media), set up a **freelance profile** on **Upwork** or **Fiverr** and start offering your services.
11. Go through your home and **sell** anything you no longer need (electronics, clothes, furniture) on **Facebook Marketplace**, **eBay**, or **Craigslist**. Aim to make at least **$100 in a week** selling items you no longer use.

12. Dedicate **1-2 hours per day** to apply for jobs. Use sites like **Indeed**, **Glassdoor**, and **LinkedIn Jobs**.
13. Focus on **temporary, part-time, or freelance jobs** to get income while you continue the search for full-time work.
14. Message at least **3-5 people** a day in your professional network (LinkedIn, past colleagues, industry groups) to ask for job leads or referrals.
15. Let them know you're looking for work, and don't be afraid to ask for help.
16. Open a separate savings account specifically for your emergency fund (even a small one).
17. Start with **\$10-\$20 a week** to begin building a safety net for future expenses.
18. **Sign up for free online courses** on **Coursera**, **edX**, or **LinkedIn Learning**. Focus on skills that are in demand (e.g., digital marketing, coding, project management). Dedicate at least **30 minutes a day** to improve or learn a new skill that will increase your employability.

Quick Wins for Immediate Results:

Gig Work: Sign up for **2-3 gig apps** today and start earning tomorrow. Even if it's just a few hours, it's money you didn't have before.

Sell Unused Items: Aim to sell **5-10 things** in the next 2 days. Start with high-value items that can bring in cash quickly.

Apply to 5 Jobs Today: Send out applications right away—focus on ones that are urgent (temp, part-time, or contract work). Set a timer for 1 hour and apply to as many as you can.

Cancel Unnecessary Subscriptions Today: Stop spending money on things you don't need immediately. **Freeze** memberships, services, and anything that's not a necessity for survival.

More Quick-Win Ideas for Immediate Cash Flow:

Street Artist / Performer

If you have any artistic talent (drawing, painting, music, or performing), consider setting up on a busy street or park and **offering your art** for tips.
Create small **sketches**, **caricatures**, or **paintings** that passersby can purchase.

Perform live music, dance, or other street performances to earn tips in high-traffic areas.

Dog Walking or Pet Sitting

Use apps like **Rover** or **Wag** to offer dog walking and pet sitting services.

Walk dogs in your neighbourhood or nearby parks. You can earn between **$15-30 per walk**.
Offer **overnight pet sitting** if you're comfortable—this can pay significantly more.

TaskRabbit (Odd Jobs)

Join TaskRabbit and offer services like **moving help**, **cleaning**, **assembling furniture**, or **delivery assistance**.

You can get paid **hourly** or per task, depending on the job. Quick tasks like **cleaning, organizing, or assembling furniture** can be completed within a few hours.

Freelance Writing / Editing

If you have a knack for writing or editing, create a profile on **Upwork**, **Fiverr**, or **Freelancer** and start offering your services.

Offer to write **blog posts**, **product descriptions**, or **social media content**. Some gigs can pay quickly, and you can often land small projects fast.

Selling Crafts or Handmade Goods

If you're crafty, start selling **handmade jewellery**, **art**, **candles**, or other items on platforms like **Etsy** or **Facebook Marketplace**.

You can also **set up a booth** at a local craft fair or farmer's market to sell your creations directly.

Flipping Items for Profit

Buy and resell items on platforms like **eBay**, **Facebook**

Marketplace, or **Poshmark**. You can often find valuable items at thrift stores or garage sales that you can flip for a profit.

Focus on **electronics**, **clothes**, or **furniture**—items that are easy to flip and sell quickly.

Rent Out a Room (Airbnb)

If you have a spare room or even a whole apartment, consider **renting it out on Airbnb**.

Short-term rentals can bring in substantial income, especially if you live in a tourist area or near major cities.

Online Surveys and Market Research

Sign up for **survey sites** like **Swagbucks**, **InboxDollars**, or **Survey Junkie**.

Though not a huge source of income, these can provide **quick cash** or gift cards for very little time investment (spend **30 minutes to an hour** a day completing surveys or watching videos).

Virtual Assistant Work

Offer **virtual assistant** services such as **email management**, **social media management**, or **research** on platforms like **Fiverr** or **Upwork**.

Businesses and entrepreneurs are always looking for affordable virtual help, and this can be a steady source of income.

Tutoring or Teaching

Offer **tutoring** in subjects you are proficient in (math, science, languages) through platforms like **Chegg Tutors**, **Wyzant**, or **Tutor.com**.

You can also consider **teaching English online** through sites like **VIPKid** or **Italki** for quick, flexible income.

Handyman Services

If you're skilled in home repairs or maintenance, offer your services locally through **Craigslist**, **Nextdoor**, or **Facebook Marketplace**.

Common jobs could include house cleaning, car cleaning, fixing **leaky faucets**, **painting rooms**, or **cleaning gutters**. If you are confident and competent use some electrical tools to fix switchboards, etc.

Cleaning Services

Offer **cleaning services** for homes or offices.
You can do **deep cleaning**, **organising**, or **move-out cleaning** for higher-paying jobs.
Advertise locally on **Nextdoor** or **Facebook groups**.

Renting Out Gear (Cameras, Equipment, etc.)
If you have camera gear, tools, or other specialised equipment, consider **renting them out** through platforms like **Fat Llama**.
You can also rent out things like **camping gear**, **electronics**, or even **party supplies**.

Affiliate Marketing or Online Sales

Start a **blog, Instagram, or YouTube channel** around a niche you're passionate about (travel, beauty, fitness, etc.) and use **affiliate links** to earn commissions on products you promote.

This won't make you immediate cash, but it's a great long-term way to start earning passive income if you have a platform already.

Photography or Event Videography

If you own a camera and have photography skills, consider offering **portrait sessions** or **event photography** (weddings, birthdays, corporate events).

Start by promoting locally through **social media** or **Nextdoor**.

Final Thoughts: Stay Agile, Stay Focused

The key to starting from zero is **maintaining flexibility** while focusing on your immediate needs (financial survival) and your long-term goals (career growth). By following these actionable steps, you can not only survive this period but also set yourself up for future success. Keep pushing forward, and remember, the job market can change quickly—staying active in your job search and continually improving your skills will keep you in the game. By following these actionable steps, you can navigate the financial challenges of unemployment with a clear and structured plan. This will help you stay focused on your job search while maintaining financial stability, reducing stress, and preparing for future success.

CHAPTER 8: TIME MANAGEMENT AND PRODUCTIVITY

Setting Job Search Goals

Setting clear job search goals is crucial for any individual navigating the complex landscape of employment opportunities. Without defined objectives, job seekers may find themselves wandering aimlessly, applying for positions without a clear sense of purpose or direction. Establishing specific, measurable, achievable, relevant, and time-bound (SMART) goals can help create a structured approach to the job search process, making it more efficient and focused.

Begin by reflecting on your career aspirations and what you hope to achieve in your next role. Are you looking for a position that offers greater responsibility, better work-life balance, or opportunities for professional growth? Identifying your core desires will help you articulate your goals more clearly. Moreover, consider the skills and experiences you bring to the table; aligning these with your goals can enhance your confidence and self-esteem, making your job search more empowering.

Once you have a clearer picture of your aspirations, break down your overarching goals into smaller, manageable tasks. For instance, if your aim is to secure a leadership role within six months, outline the steps needed to achieve this, such as updating your CV, networking with industry professionals, or acquiring new certifications.

This step-by-step approach can alleviate stress and ensure you remain focused, which is particularly beneficial for those who may struggle with mindfulness and stress management during their search.

Additionally, regularly review and adjust your goals as necessary. The job market is dynamic, and your circumstances may change along the way. Perhaps a networking opportunity arises that alters your career trajectory or a new skill becomes essential for your desired role. Being flexible and open to reassessing your goals will help maintain your motivation and commitment throughout the process.

Finally, celebrate your achievements, no matter how small they may seem. Each step you take towards your job search goals is a victory in itself. Acknowledging these milestones not only boosts your confidence but also reinforces a positive mindset. Remember, the journey of job searching is not just about landing a position; it's also about personal growth and development, which can be just as rewarding as the destination itself.

Creating an Effective Job Search Schedule

Creating an effective job search schedule is crucial for job seekers to stay organised and focused throughout their journey. A well-structured schedule not only helps in managing time efficiently but also reduces the stress associated with the job search process. By allocating specific times for various activities, such as researching job openings, networking, and preparing applications, individuals can ensure they are making consistent progress towards their goals.

It is important to start by determining how much time you can dedicate to your job search each week. This involves assessing your current commitments, whether they be personal or professional. Once you have a clear understanding of your available time, you can create a balanced schedule that includes both job search activities and self-care practices. Incorporating wellness routines, such as exercise and mindfulness, can enhance your overall well-being and keep you motivated.

In your schedule, prioritise tasks based on their importance and deadlines. For instance, allocate specific days for applying to jobs, attending networking events, and following up on applications. Creating a checklist can help you stay on track and ensure that no important steps are overlooked. Additionally, setting measurable goals for each week can provide you with a sense of accomplishment and keep you engaged in the process.

Flexibility is another key component of an effective job search schedule. While it is important to stay committed to your routine, being adaptable to changes and unexpected opportunities is equally vital. If a networking opportunity arises or a job application deadline is moved, adjust your schedule accordingly. This flexibility not only helps you seize opportunities but also reduces potential frustration and stress.

Staying Organised and Motivated

In the journey of job seeking, staying organised and motivated is essential for achieving success. Creating a structured plan with clear goals can significantly enhance your focus and efficiency. Consider utilising tools such as planners or digital apps to track your applications, interviews, and networking efforts. By maintaining an organised approach, you will be able to visualise your progress and areas that require more attention, ultimately leading to a more productive job search.

Motivation can fade during the job search process, particularly when faced with setbacks. It is crucial to cultivate a positive mindset and remind yourself of your strengths and capabilities. Setting small, achievable milestones can provide a sense of accomplishment and help sustain your motivation. Celebrate each victory, no matter how small, and use them as stepping stones towards your larger career aspirations. This practice not only boosts your confidence but also reinforces your commitment to your goals.

Finally, it is essential to balance your job search with self-care practices. Engaging in activities that promote your well-being will ensure you remain motivated and energised. Schedule time for exercise, hobbies, and relaxation to maintain a healthy work-life balance. By prioritising your well-being alongside your job search, you will foster resilience, adaptability, and a positive outlook, all of which are vital for long-term success in your career pursuits.

1. Time Management and Productivity: Practical Steps

Step 1: Set Clear Job Search Goals

Action: Define specific, measurable, achievable, relevant, and time-bound (SMART) goals for your job search.

Example: Aim to secure a leadership role within 1 year by updating your CV, networking, and acquiring a new qualification/certification or experience.

Tool/Goal: Use a goal-setting worksheet or journal to break long-term goals into weekly and daily tasks.

Step 2: Break Goals into Manageable Tasks

Action: Divide overarching goals into smaller, actionable steps.

Example: List tasks like updating your Linkedln profile, researching five companies per week, or drafting tailored cover letters.

Tool/Goal: Use a task manager, planner, or digital app to track progress and deadlines.

Step 3: Create an Effective Job Search Schedule

Action: Allocate specific times for job search activities, networking, applications, and self-care.

Example: Schedule Monday mornings for applications, Wednesday afternoons for networking, and Friday for follow-ups.

Tool/Goal: Use a calendar or planner to visualise your week and ensure consistent progress.

Step 4: Prioritise Tasks

Action: Identify which tasks are most urgent or impactful and tackle them first.

Example: Apply for jobs with approaching deadlines before networking events.

Tool/Goal: Use a prioritisation matrix (urgent vs important) to organise your daily and weekly activities.

Step 5: Stay Organised

Action: Track all job search activities, contacts, interviews, and follow-ups in one place.

Example: Maintain a spreadsheet with columns for company name, position, date applied, contact person, and follow-up notes.

Tool/Goal: Use digital tools such as Trello, Notion, or Excel for a clear overview of your search.

Step 6: Maintain Motivation

Action: Set small milestones and celebrate achievements to sustain momentum.

Example: Reward yourself for submitting five tailored applications in a week or attending a networking event.

Tool/Goal: Use a journal or app to track accomplishments and reflect on progress.

Step 7: Incorporate Mindfulness

Action: Practice mindfulness techniques to manage stress and maintain focus.

Example: Take five minutes before starting applications to meditate or do deep breathing.

Tool/Goal: Use apps like Headspace or Calm, or simply practice mindful breathing exercises at your desk.

Step 8: Balance Job Search and Self-Care

Action: Schedule time for exercise, hobbies, and relaxation alongside job search activities.

Example: Take a brisk walk after lunch or dedicate one evening per week to a hobby unrelated to work.

Tool/Goal: Incorporate self-care blocks in your calendar to maintain energy, focus, and motivation.

2. Putting It All Together: A 30-Day Time Management and Productivity Plan

Week 1: Goal Setting and Planning

Day 1: Reflect on career aspirations and define SMART goals.
Day 2: Break goals into actionable weekly and daily tasks.
Day 3: Create a job search schedule for the week.
Day 4: Prioritise tasks based on urgency and impact.
Day 5: Set up an organisation system for applications and contacts.
Day 6: Identify potential obstacles and plan strategies to overcome them.
Day 7: Review goals and schedule; adjust as needed.

Week 2: Structured Job Search Routine

Day 8: Apply for targeted roles following your schedule.
Day 9: Attend one networking event or online webinar.
Day 10: Update CV, Linkedln, or portfolio with new achievements.
Day 11: Follow up with contacts from previous networking efforts.
Day 12: Set small weekly milestones and track progress.

Day 13: Integrate a mindfulness practice before starting applications.
Day 14: Reflect on successes and challenges; adjust schedule for next week.

Week 3: Staying Organised and Motivated

Day 15: Review all applications, contacts, and deadlines.
Day 16: Celebrate small achievements and reward progress.
Day 17: Identify areas for improvement in your search process.
Day 18: Schedule check-ins with mentors or peers for guidance.
Day 19: Track networking efforts and plan follow-ups.
Day 20: Practice mindfulness or stress-relief exercises.
Day 21: Reflect on motivation levels and adjust strategies.

Week 4: Flexibility and Review

Day 22: Evaluate schedule effectiveness; make adjustments.
Day 23: Attend another networking event or informational call.
Day 24: Review upcoming application deadlines and prioritise.
Day 25: Reflect on stress management techniques; incorporate any new methods.
Day 26: Update journal or tracking system with progress and lessons learned.
Day 27: Reassess goals and refine tasks for the next month.
Day 28: Plan self-care activities and relaxation time.
Day 29: Celebrate achievements, both big and small.
Day 30: Set goals and schedule for the following month to maintain momentum.

Chapter 8: Time Management & Task Prioritisation Journal

Time management and task prioritisation are the cornerstones of a successful job search. It's easy to become overwhelmed with the sheer volume of tasks involved—applications, interviews, networking, researching companies, and more. The key to reducing stress and increasing productivity is creating a focused, strategic plan that ensures you are using your time efficiently and tackling the most impactful tasks first.
This journal will guide you through actionable steps to organise your time and prioritise your tasks effectively, so you can maximise your efforts without burning out.

1. Understand Your Time Constraints

Actionable Steps:

Assess Available Time: Start by identifying how much time you can dedicate to your job search each day and week. Be realistic about your current commitments—whether it's a full-time job, personal obligations, or other responsibilities.

Reflection Questions:

How many hours per day/week can I realistically devote to my job search?

Are there periods during the day when I am most productive (morning, afternoon, evening)?

What are my other major time commitments, and how can I work around them?

Create a Time Audit: Track your time for a few days to understand how you are currently spending your day. This will help identify wasted time or opportunities for more focused efforts.

Example Time Audit:

9:00 AM - 10:00 AM: Job search (applications, networking)
10:00 AM - 11:00 AM: Research companies/industry trends
11:00 AM - 12:00 PM: Break/other tasks
12:00 PM - 1:00 PM: Respond to LinkedIn messages
1:00 PM - 2:00 PM: Lunch break
2:00 PM - 3:00 PM: Update CV/portfolio
3:00 PM - 4:00 PM: Follow up on applications

Time	Activity

2. Identify and Prioritise Your Tasks

Actionable Steps:

List All Tasks: Write down everything you need to do in your job search. Include tasks like applying for jobs, updating your resume, networking, attending interviews, researching companies, etc.

Example Task List:
Apply for roles in marketing (2 applications per day)
Update LinkedIn and resume (one-time task)
Follow up with previous applicants and contacts (once a week)
Attend networking events (one per week)
Research 5 companies per week

Prepare for upcoming interviews (2 hours per interview)

Use the Eisenhower Matrix for Prioritisation: Categorise your tasks into four categories based on their urgency and importance.

Urgent & Important (Do Now): These tasks need to be completed immediately.
Example: Applying for jobs with tight deadlines, preparing for an interview tomorrow.

Important but Not Urgent (Schedule): These tasks are critical but can be planned for later.
Example: Updating your LinkedIn, creating a portfolio, researching companies.

Urgent but Not Important (Delegate): Tasks that can be delegated if possible, or at least minimised.
Example: Responding to general LinkedIn messages that are not related to your job search.

Neither Urgent nor Important (Eliminate or Limit): Tasks that do not add value and can be avoided.
Example: Browsing job boards aimlessly, checking email too frequently during job search time.

Action Step: Review your task list regularly, categorising them into the matrix to ensure you're tackling the most important tasks first. Regularly adjust priorities as deadlines or new opportunities arise.

3. Break Your Goals Into Actionable, Time-Bound Tasks

Actionable Steps:

Set Specific, Measurable Tasks: Instead of vague goals like "search for jobs" or "network more," create clear, actionable steps that can be measured.

Example:

Apply to three marketing roles by Friday."
Send five connection requests to professionals in the marketing field by Thursday."
Research two companies per day to apply to."

Time-Block Your Calendar: Once you've identified the key tasks, allocate specific times for them in your calendar. Time-blocking helps ensure you focus on one task at a time without distractions.

Example Time Blocking:

Monday 9:00 AM - 11:00 AM: Apply for 3 marketing roles
Monday 1:00 PM - 2:00 PM: Research 2 companies
Tuesday 9:00 AM - 11:00 AM: Update LinkedIn and resume
Tuesday 2:00 PM - 3:00 PM: Follow up with last week's applications

Action Step: Review your calendar every morning to ensure you stick to your time-blocked tasks. Adjust the schedule as necessary, but always make sure that the most critical tasks get done first.

4. Stay Accountable with Tracking & Weekly Reviews

Actionable Steps:

Track Your Daily Progress: Use a daily log to record what tasks you've completed and how much time you spent on each. This will give you insight into how well you're sticking to your plan and whether any adjustments are needed.

Example Tracking System:

Date:
Task Completed: Apply to 3 jobs
Time Spent: 1.5 hours
Notes: Successfully applied to all three jobs, one job had a short deadline

Weekly Review: At the end of each week, assess your progress and adjust your strategy for the upcoming week. What went well? What can be improved?

Weekly Reflection Questions:

Did I accomplish my priority tasks this week?

Were there any unexpected obstacles that slowed my progress?

What tasks did I under-allocate time to?

What changes can I make next week to improve my efficiency?

If you didn't apply to enough jobs, adjust your weekly goal. List adjustments you can make.

If networking didn't yield results, consider joining a new industry group or attending more events.

5. Maintain Flexibility and Adapt as Needed

Actionable Steps:

Leave Room for Flexibility: While it's crucial to have a structured plan, flexibility is equally important. Unplanned opportunities, such as spontaneous networking events or urgent job applications, will arise.

Action Step: Keep some buffer time in your schedule for unexpected opportunities or urgent tasks. For instance, if you know you'll need to spend an hour at a last-minute interview or networking event, adjust your evening tasks accordingly.

Adapt to Changing Priorities: The job market is always evolving. New opportunities might require more immediate action, while some of your previous goals might no longer be relevant. Be open to reassessing and shifting your priorities as necessary.

Example Adjustments:
If you receive an invitation for an interview, adjust your schedule to prioritise preparation.
If a job you're interested in is posted with a deadline in two days, rearrange your plan to ensure you submit your application on time.

6. Guard Against Procrastination and Distractions

Actionable Steps:

Set Timers and Limits: To avoid distractions, use the Pomodoro Technique or another time-management method that helps you stay focused. Set a timer for 25 minutes of focused work, followed by a 5-minute break.

Example Pomodoro Session:

Task: Apply for jobs
Work: 25 minutes of focused application writing
Break: 5-minute walk or stretching

Remove Distractions: Identify common distractions during your job search (e.g., social media, phone notifications) and limit them while working on priority tasks. Consider using apps like **Freedom** or **Forest** to block distracting websites during focused work sessions.

7. Practice Self-Care to Recharge and Stay Energised

Actionable Steps:

Incorporate Breaks and Downtime: Avoid working for long stretches without rest. Take breaks to recharge, walk, meditate, or engage in a hobby. Self-care ensures you don't burn out and helps maintain a positive mindset throughout your job search.

Example Breaks:

Take a 15-minute break after completing a 1-hour task. Schedule a 30-minute walk after a focused afternoon of applying for jobs.

Reflection Prompt:

How do I feel about my job search efforts this week?

Am I striking a good balance between work and rest, or do I need to make changes?

Final Thoughts:

Mastering time management and task prioritisation will empower you to navigate your job search with purpose and efficiency. By focusing on high-impact tasks, setting clear goals, and regularly reviewing your progress, you can turn the job search process into a more organised, less overwhelming experience. Remember, the way you manage your time today impacts the opportunities you're ready for tomorrow. Stay intentional, stay focused, and trust the process.

Chapter 9: Evaluation Job Offers

Understanding Job Offer Components

Understanding the components of a job offer is crucial for every job seeker. A job offer is not merely a contract; it is a comprehensive document that outlines various elements critical to your potential employment. Each component carries significant weight and can influence your decision to accept or decline the offer. Therefore, understanding these components can empower you to negotiate and secure a position that aligns with your career goals and personal values.

The first essential component of a job offer is the salary. This figure is typically presented as an annual salary or hourly wage, and understanding it in the context of your worth is vital. Consider not only the base salary but also how it compares to industry standards and your previous earnings. Additionally, reflect on how this salary will support your lifestyle and financial goals. Knowing your worth can enhance your confidence during negotiations and ensure you receive fair compensation for your skills and experience.

Benefits are another critical aspect of a job offer. These can include health insurance, retirement plans, paid leave, and other perks that can significantly affect your job satisfaction and overall well-being. As a job seeker, it's important to evaluate these benefits against your personal needs and circumstances. For instance, if you prioritise work-life balance, consider the amount of paid leave or flexible working arrangements offered.

Understanding the full spectrum of benefits can help you appreciate the value of the job beyond just the salary.

Work environment and culture also play a vital role in your decision-making process. Job offers should include details about the company's culture, values, and expectations. Assessing whether the company's ethos aligns with your personal values is essential for long-term satisfaction. Consider factors such as the management style, team dynamics, and opportunities for growth and development. A good cultural fit can significantly enhance your job satisfaction and overall happiness in the workplace.

Lastly, consider the terms of employment, including job responsibilities, performance expectations, and the duration of the contract if applicable. Understanding these terms can prevent future misunderstandings and ensure clarity in your role. As a job seeker, you should feel empowered to ask questions about any part of the offer that seems unclear. By understanding all the components of a job offer, you can make an informed decision that aligns with your career aspirations and personal values.

Negotiating Salary and Benefits

Negotiating salary and benefits is a crucial step in the job search process that can significantly impact your financial well-being and job satisfaction. As a job seeker, understanding your worth in the market is essential. Research salary ranges for your position and industry, using reputable sources to gather data. This preparation allows you to enter negotiations with confidence and clarity about what you deserve.

When it comes to negotiating, timing and approach are key. Initiate discussions about salary and benefits only after receiving a job offer, demonstrating your commitment to the role while ensuring you are in a strong position to negotiate. Articulate your value by highlighting your skills, experiences, and contributions that justify your desired compensation. This strategic approach not only showcases your professionalism but also sets the tone for a constructive dialogue.

Additionally, consider the entire compensation package, not just the salary. Benefits such as health insurance, growth opportunities, budget for training & development/upskil ling, retirement plans, and flexible work options can greatly enhance your overall job satisfaction. Tailor your negotiation strategy to include these elements, as they can significantly affect your work-life balance and financial stability. Be open to discussing various options that align with your needs and values.

Practising assertiveness is vital in these negotiations. Approach conversations with a positive mindset, focusing on collaboration rather than confrontation. Use phrases that express your enthusiasm for the role while firmly stating your expectations. This balance of confidence and openness can foster a more productive negotiation environment, increasing the likelihood of achieving a satisfactory outcome.

Finally, remember that negotiating is not just about securing the best deal; it's also about establishing a mutually beneficial relationship with your employer. Be prepared to compromise while ensuring that your core needs are met. This mindset will not only enhance your negotiation success but also lay the groundwork for a healthy working relationship moving forward.

Making the right decision for your career is a pivotal step in the journey of job seeking. It requires careful consideration of your strengths, values, and passions. Understanding what truly motivates you can help clarify the direction you wish to take. Whether you are looking to transition into a new field or advance in your current career, aligning your choices with your personal and professional goals is essential.

As a job seeker, it is important to take stock of your skills and experiences. Reflect on the roles that have brought you fulfilment and satisfaction in the past. This reflection can guide you towards opportunities that resonate with your core values. Engaging with career coaches can provide valuable insights and support in identifying the path that suits you best.

In addition to self-reflection, seeking feedback from trusted mentors or coaches can illuminate blind spots you may have. They can offer perspectives on your strengths and areas for growth, which can be crucial in making informed career choices. Embrace constructive criticism as a means to refine your approach and enhance your decision-making process.

When weighing your options, consider the long-term implications of your decisions. It is tempting to chase immediate rewards, but a strategic mindset is necessary for sustainable success. Think about how each choice aligns with your future aspirations and how it can contribute to your overall well-being and career satisfaction.

Finally, remember that making the right decision is not just about choosing the best job; it's about fostering a career that nurtures your growth and happiness.

Cultivating a mindset of resilience and adaptability will empower you to navigate challenges and seize opportunities as they arise. Ultimately, the right decision will be one that aligns with your authentic self, propelling you towards a fulfilling career journey.

1. Evaluating Job Offers: Practical Steps

Step 1: Understand Job Offer Components

Action: Review all parts of a job offer carefully, including salary, benefits, work environment, culture, and terms of employment.

Example: Compare the offered salary with industry standards, assess health benefits, flexible working options, and understand your role responsibilities.

Tool/Goal: Use a checklist to evaluate each component and identify areas that require clarification or negotiation.

Step 2: Assess Salary and Financial Value

Action: Determine whether the offered salary aligns with your worth and financial goals.

Example: Research average salaries for similar roles in your region and industry before negotiating.
Tool/Goal: Use salary research websites or reports (e.g., Glassdoor, Payscale) to benchmark your value.

Step 3: Evaluate Benefits and Perks

Action: Analyse the full range of benefits included in the offer, such as health insurance, retirement plans, leave policies, and flexible work options.

Example: Consider the number of annual leave days, parental leave policies, and professional development support offered.

Tool/Goal: Create a benefits comparison table to weigh the value of different offers or negotiate missing elements.

Step 4: Consider Work Environment and Culture

Action: Reflect on the company's values, team dynamics, and management style to determine cultural fit.

Example: Attend informal chats or ask current employees about team collaboration and leadership approach.

Tool/Goal: Use a cultural alignment questionnaire to evaluate how well the company matches your preferences.

Step 5: Clarify Terms of Employment

Action: Understand your job responsibilities, performance expectations, contract duration, and reporting lines.

Example: Ask for clarification on flexible working arrangements, probation periods, or expected deliverables.

Tool/Goal: Prepare a list of questions to discuss with HR or your potential manager before accepting the offer.

Step 6: Negotiate Salary and Benefits

Action: Approach salary and benefits discussions with confidence and a collaborative mindset.

Example: Highlight your skills and experiences to justify a higher salary or additional benefits, while remaining positive and professional.

Tool/Goal: Prepare a negotiation script and list of priorities (salary, benefits, work-life balance) to ensure productive discussions.

Step 7: Consider the Entire Compensation Package

Action: Evaluate all aspects of compensation, not just base salary, including bonuses, stock options, and flexible work arrangements.

Example: Factor in a generous pension plan or professional development allowance when comparing two job offers.

Tool/Goal: Use a weighted scoring table to rank offers based on salary, benefits, culture, and career growth potential.

Step 8: Seek Guidance and Feedback

Action: Consult mentors, career coaches, or trusted peers to gain perspective on the job offer.

Example: Share your offer details with a mentor to evaluate long-term career alignment and potential growth opportunities.

Tool/Goal: Create a pros and cons list, combining personal priorities and professional advice, to make a balanced decision.

Step 9: Make a Decision Aligned with Your Career Goals

Action: Assess how the job offer fits with your values, career aspirations, and long-term plans.

Example: Prioritise opportunities that offer meaningful work, career growth, and work-life balance over short-term financial gains.

Tool/Goal: Use a decision matrix that scores offers against your core career criteria (values, growth, salary, culture).

Step 10: Accept or Decline with Professionalism

Action: Communicate your decision politely and professionally, whether accepting or declining the offer.

Example: Send a formal acceptance email highlighting enthusiasm for the role or a gracious decline thanking them for the opportunity.

Tool/Goal: Draft standard templates for acceptance and decline to ensure clarity and professionalism in all communications.

Chapter 9:
Journal: Evaluating Job Offers and Making the Right Decision

Making the right decision when presented with a job offer is crucial for long-term career satisfaction. A job offer is not just about the salary—it encompasses many components that need to be evaluated carefully to ensure it aligns with your career goals, values, and personal life. In this journal, you will explore how to assess each component of a job offer, negotiate where necessary, and make a well-informed decision.

1. Understand Job Offer Components

Actionable Step:

When you receive a job offer, take time to review every part of it—salary, benefits, work culture, and job terms. Don't rush through it. This is a decision that will impact your life for years to come.

Key Questions to Ask Yourself:

Salary: Does this salary meet your financial needs and goals? How does it compare to industry standards and your previous earnings?

Benefits: Are the benefits aligned with your health, family, and lifestyle needs? Consider health insurance, retirement contributions, paid leave, etc.

Work Culture: Does the company's culture resonate with your values? Consider how the team interacts, the company's approach to work-life balance, and leadership style.

Terms of Employment: Are your job responsibilities and performance expectations clear? Is there room for growth or additional perks like flexible hours?

Reflection:

After reviewing the job offer, note any questions or uncertainties that arise. Create a checklist with the components that you need to address further. Identify areas for negotiation and prepare to discuss them with your potential employer.

2. Assess Your Salary and Financial Goals

Actionable Step:

Research salary ranges for your role, location, and industry. Use tools like **Glassdoor** and **Payscale** to get a sense of what others in similar positions earn. This helps you assess whether the offer meets your worth.

Key Questions to Ask Yourself:

Does the salary offered align with my financial needs?

Is it competitive within the market for my experience and skills?

Will this salary support my desired lifestyle and future financial goals?

Reflection:

If the salary is lower than expected, reflect on how much flexibility you have in your budget. Consider how much room there is for negotiation and whether the job offers other value points (like growth opportunities or work-life balance) that make up for a lower salary.

3. Evaluate the Benefits and Perks

Actionable Step:

Benefits are often overlooked in job offers, but they can be just as important as salary. Take a close look at the benefits package, including health insurance, retirement plans, vacation days, and other perks (e.g., gym memberships, bonuses, professional development).

Key Questions to Ask Yourself:

Are the health insurance plans suitable for my needs?

Does the retirement plan offer significant contributions or match?

Do the paid leave and flexible working options align with my lifestyle and work-life balance?

Are there any additional perks (e.g., remote work, professional development, parental leave) that add value?

Reflection:

Create a benefits comparison table to track what each offer provides. Weight each benefit based on your personal needs (e.g., if family health insurance is a priority, make that a key consideration). This will help you understand the true value of the offer beyond just the salary.

4. Assess the Work Environment and Culture

Actionable Step:

The work environment and culture are crucial for your long-term happiness.

A positive, supportive environment can lead to job satisfaction, while a poor fit can make you dread going to work every day. Research and reflect on the company's culture, team dynamics, and management style.

Key Questions to Ask Yourself:

Do I feel aligned with the company's values and mission?

How does the management style match my preferred way of working?

What is the general work-life balance like at this company?

Are employees supported in their personal and professional development?

Reflection:

If you're unsure about the culture, consider reaching out to current or past employees on LinkedIn or attending informal networking events to gain insight into the company's environment. Evaluate whether the company's culture fosters a positive, inclusive, and growth-oriented environment for you.

5. Clarify Terms of Employment

Actionable Step:

Ensure that you understand your role's responsibilities, the performance expectations, and the contract's duration. If there's any ambiguity, ask for clarification before proceeding.

Key Questions to Ask Yourself:

Are the job responsibilities clearly defined?

What are the performance expectations and how will I be evaluated?

Are there any probationary periods or contract terms I should be aware of?

Is the role likely to evolve or change over time, and if so, how?

Reflection:

Write down your job expectations, including what you want to achieve in the first 6 months or year. This will help you measure if the offer meets your career growth needs and whether it fits with your long-term goals.

6. Negotiate Salary and Benefits

Actionable Step:

Negotiation is an essential part of the process. Approach salary and benefit discussions with confidence, keeping in mind your worth and the value you bring to the company. Use your research and self-assessment as the basis for your negotiation.

Key Questions to Ask Yourself:

What's the minimum salary and benefits package I can accept?

What additional perks or benefits are most important to me (e.g., remote work, professional development)?

How can I present my case for a higher salary or better benefits in a way that is constructive and positive?

Reflection:

Prepare a script or talking points for negotiations. Focus on framing the conversation as a collaboration. Express enthusiasm for the role while clearly stating your needs and reasons for requesting adjustments.

7. Consider the Entire Compensation Package

Actionable Step:

When comparing job offers, consider the entire compensation package, including salary, bonuses, stock options, flexible work arrangements, and opportunities for advancement.

Key Questions to Ask Yourself:

What is the total value of the entire compensation package, not just the salary?

Does the offer include bonuses or stock options that could increase the overall value?

Are there opportunities for growth and professional development that will enhance my long-term career prospects?

Reflection:

Create a weighted scoring table or a pros and cons list to help you compare offers. Assign values to each component (e.g., salary, benefits, culture) to get a clearer picture of the total offer's worth.

8. Seek Guidance and Feedback

Actionable Step:

It's always beneficial to seek advice from trusted mentors, peers, or career coaches. Share the details of your offer with someone you respect to gain another perspective.

Key Questions to Ask Yourself:

What are the strengths and weaknesses of the offer, as viewed by a mentor or advisor?

Does the offer align with my long-term career goals and values?

Are there any red flags or missed opportunities that I might not have noticed?

Reflection:

Take feedback seriously but remember that the final decision is yours. Use it to ensure you've considered all perspectives and angles before making a decision.

9. Make a Decision Aligned with Your Career Goals

Actionable Step:

Weigh all factors and evaluate the job offer in the context of your long-term career aspirations. Consider how the role aligns with your personal values, professional growth, and future goals.

Key Questions to Ask Yourself:

How does this job align with my long-term career goals?

Does this position offer the growth opportunities I need?

Will this job contribute positively to my overall well-being, both professionally and personally?

Reflection:

Use a decision matrix to score each offer based on key factors like salary, benefits, culture, and career growth potential. This will help you make an informed decision that is best aligned with your career vision.

10. Accept or Decline with Professionalism

Actionable Step:

Once you've made your decision, communicate your choice with professionalism. Whether accepting or declining, your response should reflect gratitude and professionalism.

Key Questions to Ask Yourself:

How can I express my enthusiasm and commitment if I accept the offer?

How can I respectfully decline the offer if I choose not to accept it?

Reflection:

Draft a clear and concise email for both accepting or declining the offer. Express gratitude and professionalism in both cases. Remember, the way you decline an offer can influence your professional reputation for future opportunities.

For an entry-level role, while many of the same components are still important, you may need to adjust your expectations and focus. Entry-level roles are often stepping stones to more advanced positions, so your evaluation should include both immediate concerns (e.g., salary, benefits, and work culture) and long-term opportunities for growth and learning. Here are some additional considerations that are specifically relevant for entry-level roles:

1. Emphasise Growth and Development Opportunities

Actionable Step:

As an entry-level candidate, one of the most important aspects of your decision-making process should be the potential for professional growth. Evaluate how the company supports the development of new employees, especially in the context of skill-building, mentorship, and career advancement.

Key Questions to Ask Yourself:

Does the company offer structured training programs or onboarding processes that will help me learn quickly and effectively?

Is there a clear career progression path for someone in this role?

Does the company have a culture of promoting from within, or is advancement more externally-focused?

Are there mentorship opportunities or senior employees available to guide you?

Reflection:

Think about the skills you want to develop and whether this role will provide opportunities for learning. The most valuable thing an entry-level role can offer is a foundation for your career, so prioritise companies that invest in your growth.

2. Consider the Learning Curve

Actionable Step:

Entry-level roles often come with a steep learning curve. Assess the level of support and training the company provides to help you get up to speed.

Key Questions to Ask Yourself:

How long is the training or onboarding period?

Will there be ongoing learning or professional development opportunities available?

Is there support for asking questions and receiving feedback in a constructive manner?

Reflection:

Gauge whether the company will provide enough resources, mentorship, or training to help you feel successful in the role.

A steep learning curve can be daunting, but it's much easier to handle when you have proper support and guidance.

3. Prioritise Work-Life Balance and Flexibility

Actionable Step:

For entry-level positions, work-life balance can be a huge factor, especially as you may be balancing early career responsibilities with other personal commitments (e.g., school, side hustles, family). Evaluate the company's stance on flexible working hours, remote work options, and overall job flexibility.

Key Questions to Ask Yourself:

Are there flexible work hours or remote work options for entry-level employees?

What is the company's policy on work-life balance?

Does the company offer personal or mental health days, and are these typically utiliSed by employees?

Reflection:

While it's common for entry-level roles to involve longer hours or a learning-intensive period, it's also important to assess how the company treats work-life balance. Flexible options early in your career can help you manage your responsibilities outside of work.

4. Evaluate the Job Stability and Company Reputation

Actionable Step:

Even at an entry-level, it's important to consider the company's stability and overall reputation in the industry. Will this role provide security, or is it more of a "temporary" stop?

Key Questions to Ask Yourself:

How stable is the company in terms of its growth and financial standing?

What is the company's reputation in the industry and among former employees (e.g., on Glassdoor, LinkedIn)?

Is this position part of a growing or downsizing team?

Reflection:

Research the company's longevity and prospects. A role at a rapidly growing company may provide more chances for advancement, while a role at a company with a strong reputation can also offer better networking opportunities down the road.

5. Understand Job Security vs. Immediate Financial Needs

Actionable Step:

For many entry-level candidates, salary may be a more immediate concern than it would be for more seasoned professionals. However, think beyond just the starting salary—will the compensation meet your current financial needs, and will it grow as you progress in the company?

Key Questions to Ask Yourself:

Does the starting salary meet my immediate financial needs?

Is there room for raises or promotions after a certain period of time (e.g., after a year)?

Are there bonuses, commissions, or other performance-based pay opportunities in the future?

Reflection:

While it's important to get a fair starting salary, entry-level roles are often stepping stones. Consider how the compensation package will evolve with time and whether it will allow you to move up the career ladder.

6. Focus on Job Fit and Interests Over Prestige

Actionable Step:

At the entry level, you may be drawn to a job because of its title or company prestige.
However, it's important to focus on whether the job itself truly fits your interests and strengths.

Key Questions to Ask Yourself:

Does this role match my interests and career goals, even if the company or job title isn't the most prestigious?

Am I excited about the day-to-day work, or am I primarily motivated by the company's reputation?

Does this role give me the opportunity to develop skills that are important for my long-term career?

Reflection:

At the beginning of your career, it's often better to choose a job that gives you experience and aligns with your personal interests, rather than chasing prestige or a specific title.

7. Be Prepared for "Trial Runs"

Actionable Step:

Sometimes, entry-level jobs have a probation period or trial phase to ensure you're the right fit for the role and the company culture. Understanding the terms of this probation period will help you set expectations for success early on.

Key Questions to Ask Yourself:

What is the probation period, and what are the expectations for performance during that time?

What metrics will be used to evaluate my performance in the first few months?

What happens at the end of the probation period (i.e., permanent hire or contract extension)?

Reflection:

Be sure to clarify your responsibilities during this period and seek feedback frequently. Knowing what's expected during this "trial" phase will set you up for success.

8. Look for Opportunities to Contribute to Projects or New Initiatives

Actionable Step:

Even in an entry-level position, you may have the opportunity to contribute to special projects or initiatives that can give you more experience and visibility.

Key Questions to Ask Yourself:

Will there be opportunities to work on projects outside my core responsibilities?

How flexible is the company in allowing entry-level employees to take on extra tasks or leadership roles?

Is there room for innovation or process improvement that I can contribute to?

Reflection:

Don't be afraid to ask about additional opportunities for growth, whether it's contributing to a new project, volunteering for extra tasks, or shadowing someone in a more senior position.

9. Align the Role with Your Personal Values

Actionable Step:

While entry-level roles may not always align perfectly with your ultimate career goals, it's important to ensure the company's values align with yours. You'll be spending a significant amount of time at work, and it's crucial to feel that the company culture and ethos resonate with you.

Key Questions to Ask Yourself:

Does the company's mission align with my personal values or interests?

Do I feel passionate about the work the company does?

Are there any ethical concerns or values misalignments?

Reflection:

Even if the role is entry-level, aligning with the company's mission and culture will help you feel more engaged, motivated, and passionate about your job.

Final Reflection:

This process of evaluating job offers and negotiating your terms is not just about securing a pay-check. It's about creating a foundation for a fulfilling and sustainable career. By approaching each component with careful consideration and clarity, you can confidently make decisions that align with your goals, values, and aspirations. Remember, your career path is a long-term journey, and making the right decisions now will pay off in the years to come.

Chapter 10: Continuous Growth and Development

Setting Long-Term Career Goals

Setting long-term career goals is a pivotal step in the journey of job seekers. It provides a clear direction and serves as a motivational compass that guides individuals through the often-tumultuous waters of career development. By establishing specific, measurable, achievable, relevant, and time-bound (SMART) goals, one can create a framework that not only enhances focus but also fosters a sense of purpose in their career trajectory.

Identifying one's core values and passions is essential when setting long-term career goals. Job seekers must reflect on what truly matters to them, considering both personal and professional aspirations. This introspection not only aids in aligning career objectives with individual values but also strengthens the commitment to achieving these goals. Engaging with a life coach can significantly enhance this process, offering insights and strategies tailored to individual circumstances.

Moreover, long-term goals should be flexible and adaptable, acknowledging that the job market and personal circumstances can change. Job seekers should regularly revisit and revise their goals to ensure they remain relevant and motivating. This adaptability is particularly crucial in the fast-paced environments many professionals find themselves in today, where new opportunities and challenges frequently arise.

Networking plays a vital role in the pursuit of long-term career goals. Building relationships with mentors, peers, and industry professionals can provide invaluable guidance and support. These connections can offer insights into potential career paths and open doors to opportunities that align with one's goals. Job seekers should actively seek out networking events and platforms to expand their professional circle and leverage these relationships for career advancement.

Acknowledging the accomplishments, no matter how minor, reinforces the commitment to the broader vision and encourages persistence in the face of challenges. By maintaining a positive mindset and focusing on growth, job seekers can navigate their career paths with resilience and determination.

Lifelong Learning and Professional Development

Lifelong learning is an essential component of professional development, particularly for job seekers in today's rapidly changing job market. Embracing the philosophy of continuous learning not only enhances skills but also fosters adaptability, enabling individuals to respond effectively to new challenges and opportunities. By actively seeking knowledge and experiences, job seekers can create a robust foundation for their careers, allowing them to stand out in a competitive landscape.

Engaging in professional development can take various forms, from formal education to informal mentoring relationships. Life coaches and other professionals in the wellness and health sectors can particularly benefit from workshops and certifications that enhance their expertise.

These educational experiences not only provide valuable skills but also expand networks, connecting job seekers with like-minded individuals who share their passion for personal and professional growth.

For those in leadership and management roles, such as chiefs, directors, managers, etc. staying updated on trends and methodologies is crucial. This commitment to learning ensures that they can offer the best guidance to their clients. Moreover, it demonstrates a dedication to their craft, which can significantly boost their credibility and attractiveness to potential clients or employers. Continuous education can also empower coaches to refine their techniques, ensuring they are effective in fostering client success.

Confidence and self-esteem are integral to job seekers, and lifelong learning plays a vital role in building these attributes. By acquiring new skills and knowledge, individuals can enhance their self-worth and feel more prepared to tackle job interviews and networking opportunities. Additionally, mindfulness and stress management techniques can be integrated into their learning journey, helping to maintain a balanced approach to both personal and professional challenges.

Ultimately, lifelong learning is not just a strategy for career advancement; it is a mindset that encourages personal growth and resilience. For job seekers, embracing this mindset can transform their approach to the job market, turning the search for employment into a continuous journey of self-discovery and improvement. As they invest in their development, they not only enhance their employability but also cultivate a fulfilling professional life that aligns with their values and goals.

Staying Adaptable in a Changing Job Market

In today's rapidly evolving job market, adaptability has become a crucial skill for job seekers. The landscape of employment is constantly shifting due to technological advancements, economic changes, and evolving industry demands. As a job seeker, embracing flexibility allows you to navigate these changes effectively and seize new opportunities as they arise. This adaptability not only enhances your employability but also fosters resilience in the face of uncertainty.

To stay adaptable, it is essential to cultivate a growth mindset. This involves viewing challenges as opportunities for learning and development rather than obstacles. By adopting this perspective, you can remain open to new ideas, skills, and experiences that enhance your professional profile. Engaging in continuous learning, whether through formal education, online courses, or self-directed study, empowers you to stay relevant and competitive in your chosen field.

Networking is another vital aspect of maintaining adaptability. Building and nurturing professional relationships can provide valuable insights into industry trends and potential job openings. Attend industry-specific events, join professional organisations, and leverage social media platforms to connect with others in your field. These connections not only offer support but may also lead to unexpected opportunities that align with your career goals.

Additionally, developing a diverse skill set can significantly enhance your adaptability.

Consider acquiring skills that complement your primary expertise, making you more versatile and appealing to potential employers. For example, a life coach may benefit from learning about digital marketing or social media management, while a wellness coach might explore nutrition or fitness training. This breadth of knowledge can set you apart in a competitive job market.

Finally, practising mindfulness can aid in staying adaptable. Mindfulness techniques, such as meditation and deep breathing exercises, can help you manage stress and maintain focus during uncertain times. By fostering a calm and centred mindset, you can approach the job search process with clarity and confidence, enabling you to embrace change rather than fear it. Ultimately, cultivating adaptability is about being proactive and prepared, ensuring that you thrive in your career journey regardless of the challenges that may arise.

1. Continuous Growth and Development: Practical Steps

Step 1: Set Long-Term Career Goals

Action: Define clear, SMART (specific, measurable, achievable, relevant, time-bound) career goals that align with your values and aspirations.

Example: Decide that within five years you want to advance to a managerial role in your field or specialise in a particular niche of coaching.

Tool/Goal: Use a career roadmap or goal-setting worksheet to visualise your milestones and track progress.

Step 2: Identify Core Values and Passions

Action: Reflect on what truly motivates you and ensure your career goals align with these values.

Example: Realise that helping clients achieve personal growth is your primary motivation, guiding you to roles that involve coaching or mentorship.

Tool/Goal: Complete a values assessment or journal exercise to clarify priorities and drive purpose in your career.

Step 3: Maintain Flexibility and Adaptability

Action: Regularly review and adjust your goals to account for changes in the job market or personal circumstances.

Example: If a new technology emerges in your industry, update your skill development plan to stay competitive.

Tool/Goal: Keep a digital or physical career journal to track progress and make timely adjustments to goals.

Step 4: Network Strategically

Action: Build and maintain relationships with mentors, peers, and industry professionals to support your career growth.

Example: Attend industry conferences, online webinars, or local networking events to meet potential mentors and collaborators.

Tool/Goal: Use a contact management system or spreadsheet to track connections, follow-ups, and networking outcomes.

Step 5: Celebrate Milestones

Action: Acknowledge and reward yourself for achieving small steps towards your long-term goals.

Example: Completing a professional certification or landing a significant client counts as a milestone worth celebrating.

Tool/Goal: Maintain a milestone tracker to visualise achievements and maintain motivation.

Step 6: Engage in Lifelong Learning

Action: Continuously develop new skills and knowledge relevant to your field.

Example: Take online courses, attend workshops, or participate in mentoring programmes to stay up to date in your profession.

Tool/Goal: Use online platforms like Coursera, Linkedln Learning, or professional associations to plan and track learning activities.

Step 7: Enhance Professional Credibility

Action: Pursue certifications, workshops, or specialised training to strengthen your expertise.

Example: A traffic controller completes the latest town-panning certification to broaden their service offerings and client base. Similarly, a Thyroid or Diabetes specialist completes a course on managing such diseases with modern equipment and new dietary plans.

Tool/Goal: Maintain a professional development portfolio documenting all completed courses, certifications, and achievements.

Step 8: Stay Adaptable in a Changing Job Market

Action: Embrace flexibility and a growth mindset to navigate industry shifts and evolving job opportunities.

Example: Learn digital marketing skills to complement services related to your niche and increase employability in a competitive market.

Tool/Goal: Create a skill gap analysis and development plan to ensure your abilities remain current and versatile.

Step 9: Leverage Networking for Opportunities

Action: Use professional relationships to discover new roles, insights, and emerging trends in your industry.

Example: Connect with a former colleague who informs you about a job opening that perfectly fits your career goals.

Tool/Goal: Develop a networking calendar to schedule regular check-ins, events, and follow-ups with key contacts.

Step 10: Practice Mindfulness to Support Growth

Action: Integrate mindfulness techniques to maintain focus, reduce stress, and improve decision-making.

Example: Begin each day with a short meditation or reflection session before tackling job applications or client work.

Tool/Goal: Use mindfulness apps (e.g., Headspace, Calm) or journaling practices to track progress and maintain mental clarity.

Step 11: Foster Resilience and Self-Improvement

Action: Embrace challenges as opportunities to learn and adapt, strengthening professional and personal resilience.

Example: After receiving constructive feedback from a client, implement the suggestions to improve service delivery.

Tool/Goal: Maintain a reflective journal or progress log to document lessons learned and growth achieved over time.

Chapter 10: Journal for setting and achieving long-term career goals

Setting long-term career goals is an essential step in shaping your professional trajectory. These goals provide a roadmap for your career, guiding decisions, actions, and strategies over time. However, it's not enough to simply set these goals; you need to approach them with clarity, focus, and adaptability. This journal will help you break down actionable steps, keep track of your progress, and provide tools to ensure that your career goals are aligned with your values and aspirations.

Step 1: Set Clear, SMART Career Goals

Action:

Define long-term career goals that are Specific, Measurable, Achievable, Relevant, and Time-bound (SMART). These goals should be ambitious but realistic and directly tied to your values and desired career path.

Example:

Goal: Within five years, I want to become a senior project manager in the healthcare industry, specialising in process optimisation.

Timeframe: Achieve this role by the end of Year

Measure: Transition into the role by completing a project management certification, leading at least three significant projects, and receiving positive performance reviews.

Tracking:

Use a **career roadmap** to visualise the steps needed to achieve your goal. Break it down by year and quarter, specifying milestones.

Progress Tracker: Maintain a checklist to mark off when each smaller goal is completed.

Step 2: Identify Core Values and Passions

Action:

Reflect deeply on what truly motivates you. These values and passions should act as a compass for your career decisions and help ensure that your goals align with your authentic self.

Example:

Values: Personal growth, autonomy, and helping others.

Passion: Coaching individuals through life transitions and improving their well-being.

Tracking:

Values Assessment: Complete a personal values assessment (many are available online) to identify and prioritise your core values.

Reflection Journal: Use a dedicated journal to reflect on how your current or future roles align with your values. Revisit this journal every 3-6 months to check for any changes.

Step 3: Regularly Revisit and Adjust Your Goals

Action:

The job market and your personal circumstances will change over time. Review your goals regularly (annually or bi-annually) and adjust them as necessary to remain relevant and motivating.

Example:

If a new technology emerges that impacts your industry, you might revise your goal to include acquiring this new skill or certification.

Tracking:

Maintain a **digital or physical career journal** to track your goals, document any adjustments, and note reasons for changes.

Step 4: Build a Strategic Network

Action:

Networking is a powerful tool for career advancement. Focus on building meaningful, professional relationships with mentors, peers, and industry leaders who can provide guidance, support, and new opportunities.

Example:

Attend at least two industry conferences or webinars per year.

Connect with professionals on LinkedIn and aim to engage with them by commenting on posts or sharing valuable content.

Tracking:

Networking Tracker: Keep a spreadsheet or use a CRM (like HubSpot) to record your professional connections. Track follow-up dates and outcomes of each interaction.

Monthly Check-Ins: Allocate time once a month to engage with a mentor or expand your network via social media or in-person events.

Step 5: Celebrate Milestones and Small Wins

Action:

Recognise and celebrate your achievements, no matter how small. Every milestone you reach brings you closer to your long-term goals and should be acknowledged to keep your motivation high.

Example:

Completing a certification course.
Securing a speaking opportunity at a local event.
Getting positive feedback from a colleague or client.

Reflection Journal: After each celebration, journal about how it feels and the impact it has on your larger goals.

Step 6: Engage in Lifelong Learning

Action:

Make continuous learning a habit. Whether through formal education, certifications, online courses, or mentoring, ensure you're constantly updating and expanding your skill set to stay competitive.

Example:

Enroll in a course related to your career advancement (e.g., project management, advanced leadership, etc.).

Join a community or professional group to learn from others in your field.

Tracking:

Learning Log: Maintain a log of courses, workshops, and books you've completed or read. Record key takeaways and how they apply to your career development.

Learning Goals: Set a target of at least one major learning experience per quarter, whether it's a course, seminar, or new book.

Step 7: Enhance Professional Credibility

Action:

Build your credibility by pursuing certifications, workshops, and specialised training that will elevate your expertise and make you more marketable.

Example:

Obtain certification in a recognised industry standard (e.g., PMP for project managers, certification in a relevant software tool, etc.).

Volunteer to lead projects or initiatives at work to demonstrate your skills.

Where can you volunteer and at what position that aligns with your long term career goals?

Tracking:

Certification Tracker: Keep track of certifications, their renewal dates, and any new qualifications you aim to obtain.

Portfolio Development: Build a professional portfolio to document your certifications, skills, and accomplishments, especially if you're in a field that requires tangible proof of your work.

Step 8: Stay Adaptable in a Changing Job Market

Action:

Adapt to the ever-changing job landscape by staying flexible, seeking new skills, and embracing a growth mindset.

Example:

Learn new tools or software that become popular in your industry.
Be open to new job opportunities that may not have been on your radar initially but could provide valuable experience.

Tracking:

Skill Gap Analysis: Regularly analyse the skills you have versus those required in your field. Create a development plan to close any gaps.

Flexibility Journal: Note any instances where you adapted to a new opportunity or skill set, and track how it influenced your career trajectory.

Step 9: Leverage Networking for Opportunities

Action:

Use your network to discover new career opportunities and gain insights into industry trends that may affect your long-term goals.

Example:

Connect with a colleague from a previous job who informs you of a role that aligns with your goals.

Leverage your network to ask for feedback on your resume or interview techniques.

Tracking:

Networking Outcome Tracker: Keep notes on all professional interactions, including any job leads or advice received.

Follow-Up Plan: Have a system in place for following up with key contacts after an event or meeting. Track this in a calendar to maintain momentum.

Step 10: Practice Mindfulness to Support Growth

Action:

Incorporate mindfulness practices into your daily routine to reduce stress, maintain focus, and improve decision-making as you pursue your career goals.

Example:

Start your day with a 10-minute meditation session before tackling work or job applications.

Use deep breathing exercises to manage stress during interviews or high-pressure situations.

Tracking:

Mindfulness Log: Keep a journal where you track your mindfulness practices (e.g., meditation, journaling, breathing exercises) and how they contribute to your overall well-being and professional focus.

Wellness Goals: Set specific goals, like practicing mindfulness for 5 minutes a day, and gradually increase the time spent on these activities as you become more comfortable.

Step 11: Foster Resilience and Self-Improvement

Action:

Embrace challenges as opportunities to learn and grow. Develop resilience by reflecting on feedback, learning from mistakes, and continually improving.

Example:

After receiving constructive feedback, adjust your approach and track the positive changes in your performance.

Reflect on a recent failure and identify the lessons learned and how it contributes to your career growth.

Tracking:

Resilience Tracker: Log challenges, feedback, and how you responded to them. Use this as a source of strength during tough times.

Challenges	Response

Self-Improvement Journal: Write down your experiences of overcoming adversity and how each experience contributed to your personal and professional growth.

Conclusion: Creating a Continuous Cycle of Growth

Achieving long-term career goals requires a mix of planning, flexibility, and constant self-reflection. By using these actionable steps and tracking methods, you can stay on course, adapt to changes, and celebrate your progress along the way. The key is to remain focused on your values, continue learning, and leverage your network as you build the career you desire. With persistence, resilience, and a strategic approach, you can transform your career goals into a fulfilling reality.

Ready to Land Your Dream Job?

Thank you for taking the time to read this book and investing in your career growth. The path to professional success is a continuous one, and I'm here to support you in reaching your goals. If you found this book helpful, I invite you to join me at one of my upcoming practical workshops and seminars.

These sessions are designed to equip you with the skills, strategies, and tools you need to succeed in your job search. Unlike traditional training, my workshops are hands-on and action-oriented, offering you ready-to-use templates for CVs, Cover Letters, and more.

What you will get: Ready-to-use Templates:

CVs, Cover Letters, and more designed to grab employer's attention immediately.

Linkedln Profile optimization - Create a standout Linkedln profile and practically learn how to network for opportunities.

Interview Mastery - Tips and techniques to ace interviews, including virtual interview strategies.

Networking Skills - Learn how to leverage connections that lead to job offers.
You'll leave with practical tools, take-home resources, and a clear, actionable job search plan to move forward with confidence.

Why You Can't Miss This Workshop?

Real-World Tools & Resources: Leave with practical tools, templates, and a clear plan to execute your job search strategy.

Global Reach: Whether you want a job in your local area or across borders, we'll show you how to tap into global opportunities.

Confidence & Clarity: Say goodbye to confusion and second-guessing. You'll leave with the confidence and knowledge you need to succeed.

This Workshop is Perfect for You If:

You've been struggling to find the right job or transition into a new career.
You want a more effective, strategic approach to job searching.
You're ready to tap into global or remote job opportunities.

Don't wait any longer. Transform your job search into a results-driven journey.

Join the Job Search GPS Workshop and take the first step toward landing your dream job—anywhere in the world. Sign up today at www.aeronskills.co.nz or contact us at info@aeronskills.co.nz to reserve your spot!

Final Thoughts:

As you embark on your job search journey, remember that the path to success is not always linear. The strategies outlined in this book are designed to empower you, but the real work lies in your hands. Stay resilient, stay focused, and continue building upon your personal and professional growth. This journey is an opportunity to not only secure a job but to shape the career and life you truly desire.